SPANISH
SUPER REVIEW®

By the Staff of
Research & Education Association

Research & Education Association
Visit our website at: www.rea.com

Research & Education Association
61 Ethel Road West
Piscataway, New Jersey 08854
E-mail: info@rea.com

SPANISH SUPER REVIEW®

Printed in the United States of America

Library of Congress Control Number 2013932758

ISBN-13: 978-0-7386-1120-4
ISBN-10: 0-7386-1120-4

SUPER REVIEW® and REA® are registered trademarks
of Research & Education Association, Inc.

REA's *Spanish Super Review*®

Need help with Spanish? Want a quick review or refresher for class? This is the book for you!

REA's *Spanish Super Review*® gives you everything you need to know!

This *Super Review*® can be used as a supplement to your high school or college textbook, or as a handy guide for anyone who needs a fast review of the subject.

- **Comprehensive, yet concise coverage** – review covers the material that is typically taught in a beginning-level Spanish course. Each topic is presented in a clear and easy-to-understand format that makes learning easier.

- **Questions and answers for each topic** – let you practice what you've learned and build your Spanish skills.

- **End-of-chapter quizzes** – gauge your understanding of important Spanish language concepts, so you'll be ready for any assignment, quiz, or test.

Whether you need a quick refresher on the subject, or are prepping for your next test, we think you'll agree that REA's *Super Review*® provides all you need to know!

Available Super Review® Titles

ARTS/HUMANITIES
Basic Music
Classical Mythology
History of Architecture
History of Greek Art

BUSINESS
Accounting
Macroeconomics
Microeconomics

COMPUTER SCIENCE
C++
Java

HISTORY
Canadian History
European History
United States History

LANGUAGES
English
French
French Verbs
Italian
Japanese for Beginners
Japanese Verbs
Latin
Spanish

MATHEMATICS
Algebra & Trigonometry
Basic Math & Pre-Algebra
Calculus
Geometry
Linear Algebra
Pre-Calculus
Statistics

SCIENCES
Anatomy & Physiology
Biology
Chemistry
Entomology
Geology
Microbiology
Organic Chemistry I & II
Physics

SOCIAL SCIENCES
Psychology I & II
Sociology

WRITING
College & University Writing

About Research & Education Association

Founded in 1959, Research & Education Association (REA) is dedicated to publishing the finest and most effective educational materials—including study guides and test preps—for students in middle school, high school, college, graduate school, and beyond.

Today, REA's wide-ranging catalog is a leading resource for teachers, students, and professionals. Visit *www.rea.com* to see a complete listing of all our titles.

Acknowledgments

We would like to thank Pam Weston, Publisher, for setting the quality standards for production integrity and managing the publication to completion; Larry B. Kling, Vice President, Editorial, for his supervision of revisions and overall direction; Kelli Wilkins, Copywriter, for coordinating development of this edition; PreMedia Global, for their editorial review and revisions; Transcend Creative Services, for typesetting this edition; and Christine Saul, Senior Graphic Designer, for designing our cover.

Contents

CHAPTER 1

Alphabet and Sounds

1.1 The Alphabet

Spanish uses the same Latin alphabet as English except for the addition of four letters:

ch pronounced like "ch" in "chief"

ll pronounced like the "y" in "beyond"

ñ pronounced like "ni" in "opinion"

rr pronounced as a trilled or "rolling" sound (no English equivalent)

1.2 Consonants

c sounds like "s" before "e" and "i," and like "k" in all other cases.

g sounds like the "h" in "humid" before "e" and "i," and like the "g" in "go" or "get" in front of "a," "o," and "u." In order to obtain the hard sound before "e" and "i," Spanish interpolates the vowel "u": *guerra, guión.* In these cases the "u" is silent; a dieresis indicates that it must be pronounced: *vergüenza, güero.*

h is always silent: *ahora, húmedo, horrible.*

v is pronounced like "b" in all cases.

y sounds like "ll" at the beginning of a word or syllable. When it stands alone or comes at the end of a word, it is equivalent to the vowel "i."

z is pronounced like "s."

(This pronunciation guide follows Latin American usage. In Castilian Spanish the soft "c" and the "z" are pronounced like "th" in "thin.")

Letter		Spanish Example	English Example
b	[b]	*bomba*	boy
c	[k]	*calco*	keep
	[s]	*cero*	same
ch	[tʃ]	*mucho*	chocolate
d	[d]	*andar*	dog
f	[f]	*fama*	fake
g	[x]	*general*	humid
	[g]	*rango*	get
h	always silent	*hombre*	honor
j	[x]	*justo*	humid
k	[k]	*kilogramo*	kite
l	[l]	*letra*	light
ll	[ʎ]	*ella*	beyond
m	[m]	*mano*	mad
n	[n]	*pan*	no
ñ	[ŋ]	*uña*	onion
p	[p]	*padre*	poke
q	[k]	*que*	kite
r	[r]	*pero*	(These have a flap sound and a trilled or
rr	[rr]	*perro*	"rolling" sound with no English equivalent.)
s	[s]	*casa*	some
t	[t]	*patata*	tame
v	[b]	*vamos*	boy
x	[ks]	*máximo*	fox
y	[j]	*yo*	yes
z	[s]	*zapato*	same

1.3   Vowels

The sounds of the Spanish vowels are invariable.

a   sounds approximately like "a" in "ah."

e   sounds approximately like "e" in "men."

i   sounds approximately like "ee" in "eel."

o   sounds approximately like "o" in "or."

u   sounds approximately like "oo" in "moon."

Letter		Spanish Example	English Example
a	[a]	*pata*	father
e	[e]	*pelo*	men
i	[i]	*filo*	eel
o	[o]	*poco*	or
u	[u]	*luna*	moon

1.3.1   Diphthongs

A combination of one strong (*a, e, o*) and one weak vowel (*i, u*) or of two weak ones is a diphthong and counts as one syllable:

ai, ay	*aire, hay*	pronounce like "eye"
ei, ey	*reino, ley*	pronounce like "may"
oi, oy	*oigo, hoy*	pronounce like "toy"
iu	*triunfo*	pronounce like "you"
ui, uy	*cuidar, muy*	pronounce like "Louie"
ue	*hueso, muerte*	pronounce like "west"

1.4   Stress and Accent Marks

There are two basic rules that indicate stress in Spanish. If either of these two rules is broken, a written accent mark will appear over the word.

a. If a word ends in a vowel, *-n*, or *-s*, the normal stress is on the *penultimate* (next to last) syllable.

esposa (over the *o*)
clase (over the *a*)
crimen (over the *i*)

b. If a word ends in any other letter (than those mentioned above), the normal stress will fall on the last syllable.

hablar (over the second *a*)
papel (over the *e*)
nivel (over the *e*)

c. Some one-syllable words will be accented according to their grammatical functions.

mi (possessive adjective) vs. *mí* (prepositional pronoun)
mas (**but**—conjunction) vs. *más* (**more**—adverb)
si (if) vs. *sí* (**yes**)
se (reflexive pronoun) vs. *sé* (I **know**—verb)
tu (possessive adjective) vs. *tú* (subject pronoun)
el (article) vs. *él* (subject pronoun)

One-syllable words may or may not have written accents depending on their grammatical functions: *sí* (affirmative pronoun, "yes")/*si* (conjunction, "if"); *dé* (verb)/*de* (preposition); *él* (pronoun)/*el* (article); *tú* (pronoun, "you")/*tu* (possessive adjective, "your").

1.5   Syllabic Division

• A consonant between two vowels joins the second vowel to form a syllable: *li-te-ra-tu-ra, e-ne-mi-go, a-ho-ra*;

• two consonants together must be separated: *cuer-no, pac-to*;

• "*ch*," "*ll*," and "*rr*" are considered one letter and are not separated;

• "*l*" and "*r*" preceded by "*b*," "*c*," "*d*," "*f*," "*g*," "*p*," or "*t*" are not separated: *ha-blar, a-brup-to, te-cla, pul-cri-tud, me-lo-dra-ma, in-flu-yo, a-gra-de-cer*;

- "*ns*" and "*bs*" are not separated in groups of three or four consonants: *ins-cri-bir, obs-tá-cu-lo*;

- in words formed with prefixes, the prefix stands alone as one syllable: *sub-ra-yar; in-ú-til, des-a-gra-dar.*

Problem Solving Examples:

Select the correct word forms:

A (**mi/mí**) me gusta (**mas/más**) (**mi/mí**) idea que la suya.

(**Si/Sí**) quiere ir con ellos, es mejor que les diga que (**si/sí**).

Yo no (**se/sé**) lo que (**tu/tú**) quieres hacer con (**tu/tú**) vida.

Ella no esperaba que (**el/él**) le regalase (**el/él**) reloj a ella.

mí, más, mi; Si, sí; sé, tú, tu; él, el.

I like my idea better than his/hers/yours/theirs.

If he wants to go with them, it's better to tell them yes.

I don't know what you want to do with your life.

She wasn't expecting that he would give her the watch.

Mí with an accent mark is a prepositional pronoun. *Mi* without an accent mark is a possessive adjective. *Más* is the correct response because the accent mark signifies the adverb meaning "more." *Si* with no accent mark means "if," but *sí* with an accent mark means "yes." The first person singular form of *saber* is *sé* and means "I know." *Tú* with an accent mark is the informal subject pronoun "you." *Tu* without an accent mark is a possessive adjective. *El* without an accent mark is simply a masculine article, while *él* with an accent mark is the subject pronoun that means "he."

Underline the stressed syllables and then add the written accents:

A Pedro le gusta mucho el cafe de esta cafeteria pero no le gusta el pastel que esta comiendo ahora. Prefiere los bocadillos de jamon.

A A <u>Pe</u>dro le <u>gus</u>ta <u>mu</u>cho el ca<u>fé</u> de <u>es</u>ta cafete<u>rí</u>a <u>pe</u>ro no le <u>gus</u>ta el pas<u>tel</u> que es<u>tá</u> co<u>mien</u>do a<u>ho</u>ra. Pre<u>fie</u>re los boca<u>di</u>llos de ja<u>món</u>.

Pedro likes the coffee from this cafeteria but he doesn't like the pastry he's eating now. He prefers the ham sandwiches.

A word ending in a vowel, -*n*, or -*s* stressed in the last syllable will receive a written accent (*ca-fé, es-tá, ja-món*) because it has broken rule a in Section 1.4. Also, when a weak vowel and a strong vowel go together and the weak vowel (*i, u*) needs to be stressed, it will have a written accent, regardless of the position it has in the word (for example: *ca-fe-te-rí-a*).

CHAPTER 2

Articles

2.1 Forms of the Definite Article

The forms of the definite article are:

	Masculine	Feminine
Singular	*el*	*la*
Plural	*los*	*las*

2.1.1 Masculine Article with Feminine Nouns

El is used instead of *la* before feminine nouns beginning with stressed "*a*" or "*ha*": *el agua, el hacha, el alma, el hambre.*

2.1.2 Contractions

El contracts to *al* when the article follows the preposition *a* (*a* + *el*) and to *del* when the article follows the preposition *de* (*de* + *el*).

2.2 Uses of the Definite Article

The definite article is used in Spanish (but not in English):

- when the noun represents an abstraction: **life** is short; **time** is money; **freedom** is worth fighting for; **politics** is a practical art. (In Spanish: *la vida, el tiempo, la libertad, la política.*)

- when the noun includes the totality of a category: **books** are good; **man** is mortal; the Incas were acquainted with **gold**; **bread** is a staple. (In Spanish: *los libros, el hombre, el oro, el pan*);

- with the days of the week (except after a form of the verb *ser*) and the seasons of the year: *el lunes* (but *hoy es lunes*); *la primavera, el otoño;*

- with the hours of the day: *son las tres de la tarde; a las doce del día* (or *al mediodía*);

- with personal or professional forms of address in the third person: *el señor Jiménez, la señorita Méndez, el doctor Márquez, el licenciado Vidriera.* (It is omitted when the individual is directly addressed and in front of titles such as *Don, Doña, San,* or *Santo[a]: venga, señor Jiménez; no se preocupe, señorita Méndez*);

- with the parts of the body or articles of clothing instead of the possessive adjective: I brushed **my** teeth. *Me cepillé los dientes.* I put on **my** shirt. *Me puse la camisa;*

- with the names of languages except after the prepositions *en* and *de* and the verb *hablar: el francés es difícil* (but *no hablo francés; ese texto está en francés*).

2.3   The Neuter Article *Lo*

The neuter article is neither feminine nor masculine. In Spanish this is expressed by *lo* (which can also be used as the masculine direct object). However, as the neuter article, it remains invariable exclusively in the singular and is used as follows:

a.   *lo* + adjective = part/thing

  lo importante   the important part/thing
  lo mejor   the best part/thing

b.   *lo* = adj/adv + *que* = how

Tú no sabes lo importante que *es.*
You don't know **how** important it is.

Ella no entiende lo cansadas que *estamos.*
She doesn't know **how** tired we are.

2.4   Forms of the Indefinite Article

The indefinite article must agree in gender and number with the noun it modifies. Its forms are the following:

	Masculine	Feminine
Singular	*un*	*una*
Plural	*unos*	*unas*

*   *un perro*—a dog

*   *unos perros*—some dogs

Note that feminine nouns beginning with a stressed "a" or "ha" take *un* instead of *una*: ***un** alma,* ***un** hacha,* ***un** hada madrina.* This rule only applies if the noun is singular.

2.5   Uses of the Indefinite Article

In the following cases, the indefinite article is omitted in Spanish (but not in English):

*   after the verb *ser* with nouns denoting profession, religion, or nationality: *soy profesor, son católicos, es argentina.* (This rule does not apply when the noun is followed by an adjective or some other modifier: *soy **un** profesor exigente*);

*   with words such as *otro* (other), *medio* (half), *cien* (one hundred or a hundred), *mil* (one thousand or a thousand): *tengo otro amigo en el país; mide un metro y medio; cuesta mil dólares.*

Problem Solving Examples:

 Make the correct choices:

No vamos (**a el/al**) cine; vamos (**a la/ala**) playa.

Esa casa es (**de el/del**) amigo (**de los/delos**) vecinos.

(**El/La**) agua de esa fuente no se puede beber.

 al, a la; del, de los; El.

We're not going to the movies; we're going to the beach.

That house is the neighbors' friend's.

The water from that fountain cannot be drunk.

Only the masculine singular article *el* contracts to *al/del* when preceded by the prepositions *a/de*. A feminine noun beginning with a stressed *a/ha* must use the masculine article *el/un* when the noun is used in its singular form. In the plural, the feminine article is used.

 Complete with the correct definite/indefinite articles or leave blank, as needed:

_____ hijo mayor de Juan tiene _____ bicicleta como ésta.

Juan's oldest son has a bike like this one.

_____ mejor es que no vayas a _____ nuestra casa.

The best thing is for you not to go to our house.

_____ señora Suárez llega _____ martes a _____ una.

Mrs. Suárez arrives on Tuesday at 1:00.

Susana no es banquera; es _____ profesora de _____ italiano.

Susana is not a banker; she is an Italian teacher.

A   El, una; Lo, _____; La, el, la; _____, _____.

The definite article is used with *hijo mayor* because we are referring to a specific entity. On the contrary, *bicicleta* requires the indefinite article in this context. *Lo mejor* translates to "the best thing" and is always used with the neuter article *lo*. When a possessive adjective precedes a noun, the article cannot be used. The forms *señor*, *señorita*, etc., require the use of an article except when they are used as vocatives. The days of the week require the masculine article and the hours require the feminine one. The article must be omitted before nouns followed by the verb *ser* and denoting profession or nationality. The article is also omitted before names of languages preceded by the preposition *de*.

CHAPTER 3

Nouns

3.1 Gender

In Spanish, nouns are either masculine or feminine. Most nouns ending in *-o* or *-or* are masculine and most of those ending in *-a* or *-d* are feminine.

Masculine	Feminine
el calor—heat	*la vida*—life
el dinero—money	*la rosa*—rose
el amor—love	*la jaula*—cage
el otoño—fall	*la verdad*—truth

Many masculine nouns become feminine by changing the *-o* ending to *-a* or by adding an *-a* if the word ends in a consonant.

Masculine	Feminine
el escritor—the writer (male)	*la escritora*—the writer (female)
el doctor—the doctor (male)	*la doctora*—the doctor (female)
el hijo—the son	*la hija*—the daughter
el muchacho—the young man	*la muchacha*—the young woman

3.1.1 Exceptions

A few common words ending in -*o* are feminine:

la mano—the hand
la foto (*la fotografía*)—the photo, picture
la moto (*la motocicleta*)—the motorcycle

Likewise, some words ending in -*a* are masculine: *el día*—the day.

The majority of words ending in -*ma*, -*pa*, -*ta* are masculine:

el poema—the poem	*el poeta*—the poet
el drama—the play, drama	*el problema*—the problem
el fantasma—the ghost	*el mapa*—the map
el idioma—the language	

There are also ways of forming the feminine other than by adding an -*a* ending:

Masculine	Feminine
el rey—the king	*la reina*—the queen
el actor—the actor	*la actriz*—the actress
el poeta—the poet (male)	*la poetisa*—the poet (female)
el gallo—the rooster	*la gallina*—the hen

Sometimes the masculine and feminine words corresponding to a matched pair of concepts are different:

Masculine	Feminine
el yerno—the son-in-law	*la nuera*—the daughter-in-law
el macho—the male	*la hembra*—the female
el toro—the bull	*la vaca*—the cow

3.1.2 Nouns of Invariable Gender

Some nouns can be either masculine or feminine depending on their context or reference, without undergoing any formal alterations.

Masculine	Feminine
el artista—the artist (male)	*la artista*—the artist (female)
el estudiante—the student (male)	*la estudiante*—the student (female)
el joven—the young man	*la joven*—the young woman

3.1.3 Gender and Meaning Change

There are nouns that have different meanings depending on whether they are used as masculine or feminine:

el policía—the policeman	*la policía*—the police (force)
el Papa—the Pope	*la papa*—the potato
el cometa—the comet	*la cometa*—the kite
el orden—order (as in public order)	*la orden*—the order (to do something)
el cura—the priest	*la cura*—the cure
el guía—the guide (person)	*la guía*—the guide (book, as in *guía de teléfonos*)
el frente—the front	*la frente*—the forehead

3.2 Number

In Spanish, as in English, nouns can be singular or plural.

The most common way to form the plural is by adding the *-s* ending to the singular form of the word. (Note that the following examples are words ending in unstressed vowels.)

Singular	Plural
hombre—man	*hombres*—men
niño—boy	*niños*—boys
perro—dog	*perros*—dogs

3.2.1 Formation of the Plural by Addition of -es

In other cases (words ending in consonants or in stressed vowels other than -*é*), the plural is formed by adding an -*es* ending to the singular form of the word:

Singular	Plural
mujer—woman	*mujeres*—women
razón—reason	*razones**—reasons
jabalí—boar	*jabalíes*—boars
nuez—nut	*nueces***—nuts

Exceptions: *mamá* (mother), pl. *mamás*; *ley* (law), pl. *leyes*.

*Note that **razón** does not need an accent mark in the plural form **razones** because when a word ends in -*s* the normal stress is on the penultimate syllable.

**Note the spelling change from "*z*" to "*c*."

3.2.2 Nouns of Invariable Number

Nouns ending in -*s* are the same in the singular and the plural if the final syllable is unstressed:

el (los) rascacielos	the skyscraper(s)
el (los) paraguas	the umbrella(s)
el (los) lunes	Monday(s)

3.3 Diminutives

The Spanish endings -*ito*, -*cito*, and their feminine forms are used to indicate affection or to emphasize smallness:

*Tú eres mi **amor**.* You are my **love**.
*Tú eres mi **amorcito**.* You are my **sweetheart**.

*Quiero chocolate. Dame un **poco**.* I want chocolate. Give me **some**.
*Quiero chocolate. Dame un **poquito**.* I want chocolate. Give me **a little**.

*Ese **hombre** tiene buen aspecto.* That **man** is good looking.
*Ese **hombrecito** debe ser muy desgraciado.* That **poor man** must be very unfortunate.

3.4 Augmentatives

The endings -*ote*, -*ón*, and -*ona* are added to express increased size:

hombre—man	*hombrón*—big man
mujer—woman	*mujerona*—big woman
casa—house	*casona*—big house

Problem Solving Examples:

Q

Fill in the blanks with the correct forms of the definite article:

_____ tema de _____ canción expresa _____ amor de su autor hacia _____ libertad y _____ emoción que en él despierta _____ naturaleza.

En _____ foto que hicimos _____ día que te fuiste, sólo se ve _____ mano derecha de Paula.

El, la, el, la, la, la; la, el, la.

The theme of the song expresses the author's love for liberty and the emotion that nature awakens in him.

In the photo we took the day you went away, one only sees Paula's right hand.

Words ending in *-a*, *-d*, and *-ión* are generally feminine (*canción, libertad, emoción, naturaleza*). However, there are some exceptions (for example *el día, el tema*). Words ending in *-o* or *-or* are usually masculine (*el amor*), but there are also exceptions to this rule, such as *la foto* and *la mano*.

 Form the plurals of the following words:

hombre:	paraguas:
mujer:	papá:
miércoles:	francés:
café:	sabor:

 hombres, paraguas, mujeres, papás, miércoles, franceses, cafés, sabores.

Words ending in consonants form their plurals by adding *-es* (*mujeres, franceses, sabores*). Words ending in stressed vowels other than *-é* will generally add *-es* in their plurals; the word *papás* is one of the exceptions to this rule. Some words, such as *paraguas* or *miércoles*, have the same form in the singular and in the plural (*el paraguas/los paraguas*; *el miércoles/los miércoles*).

Quiz: Alphabet and Sounds–Nouns

1. Martín llegó a _____ universidad lleno de esperanzas.

   (A) este
   (B) el
   (C) la
   (D) nuestras

2. Hijo, ponte _____ abrigo antes de salir porque hace mucho frío y no quiero que te enfermes.

   (A) el
   (B) tu
   (C) tus
   (D) la

3. _____ problemas de encontrar otro apartamento les parecían enormes.

   (A) El
   (B) Las
   (C) Unas
   (D) Los

4. El estudiante Francisco y la _____ Ana están aprobados.

   (A) estudianta
   (B) estudiantes
   (C) estudiante
   (D) estudiantas

5. Todas esas _____ que le das, le resultan inútiles.

   (A) razón
   (B) razones
   (C) razonas
   (D) raciones

6. ¿Has visto la enorme _____ en la que viven?

   (A) casona
   (B) casísima
   (C) casina
   (D) casita

7. _____ llevó a los niños al cine.

    (A) La abuelita   (C) La abuelota

    (B) La abuelisa   (D) La abuelísima

8. _____ arma de fuego es peligrosa.

    (A) El   (C) Los

    (B) La   (D) Las

9. Ayer vimos _____ señorita Corrales.

    (A) a la   (C) a

    (B) la   (D) la a

10. ¿Estas llaves son tuyas? —No, no _____ son.

    (A) las   (C) ellas

    (B) lo   (D) nothing needed

ANSWER KEY

1. (C)	6. (A)
2. (A)	7. (A)
3. (D)	8. (A)
4. (C)	9. (A)
5. (B)	10. (B)

CHAPTER 4

Adjectives

4.1 Gender

Adjectives agree in gender and number with the nouns they modify.

a) Adjectives ending in *-o* change their ending to *-a* when they modify a feminine noun:

rubio, rubia—blond; *gordo, gorda*—fat; *bello, bella*—beautiful

Note: Some adjectives ending in *-o* drop the *-o* in front of a masculine singular noun:

bueno, buen—good

b) Adjectives ending in *-or* (or *-ón* or *-án*) add an *-a* to become feminine:

hablador, habladora—talkative

Exceptions:

mejor—better   *peor*—worse
superior—upper, superior   *inferior*—lower, inferior
exterior—outer, external   *interior*—inner, internal
anterior—earlier, anterior   *posterior*—later, posterior

c) Most other adjectives have the same ending for both genders:

verde—green	*grande*—big, great
azul—blue	*frágil*—fragile
cortés—courteous	*soez*—mean, vile

d) Adjectives of nationality each have four forms:

alemán, alemana, alemanes, alemanas
francés, francesa, franceses, francesas

> **Note**: The accent is dropped in all forms but the masculine singular.

4.2 Number

a) Adjectives ending in vowels add *-s* to form the plural:

bello, bellos—beautiful; *grande, grandes*—big, great

b) Adjectives ending in consonants add *-es* to form the plural:

azul, azules—blue; *débil, débiles*—weak; *vulgar, vulgares*—vulgar

c) If an adjective modifies more than one noun and one of those nouns is masculine, the adjective must be **masculine** and **plural**:

*Mis tíos y tías eran **ricos**.* My uncles and aunts were **rich**.
*Los hombres y las mujeres son **viejos**.* The men and women are **old**.

4.3 Shortening of Adjectives

A number of common adjectives drop either the final vowel or the final syllable.

a) The following adjectives drop the final vowel **before** a masculine singular noun or combination of adjective and masculine noun.

alguno	*algún*	(some)	*algún escritor*
ninguno	*ningún*	(no)	*ningún día*
uno	*un*	(a, an)	*un libro*

primero	primer	(first)	el primer chico
tercero	tercer	(third)	el tercer ejemplo
bueno	buen	(good)	un buen choque
malo	mal	(bad)	un mal niño

b) **Grande** becomes **gran** before any singular noun. Its meaning changes to **great** in this position.

una gran mujer	vs.	unas grandes mujeres
un gran soldado	vs.	unos grandes soldados

c) **Ciento** becomes **cien** before any plural noun or any number larger than 100 (**mil, millones**).

cien casas	100 houses
cien millones de dólares	100 million dollars

d) *Santo* becomes *San* before all male saints except ones beginning with *To* or *Do*: **San Juan, San Diego, Santo Domingo**. It also has a feminine form: **Santa Teresa**.

4.4 Qualifying Adjectives

Qualifying adjectives usually follow nouns:

un día *frío*—a **cold** day
unas sábanas *limpias*—some **clean** sheets

4.4.1 Change of Meaning with Location

Some common adjectives change their meaning with their location:

el hombre *pobre*—the poor man (having no money)
el *pobre* hombre—the poor man (pitiable)

el policía *mismo*—the policeman himself
el *mismo* policía—the same policeman

mi amigo *viejo*—my old (aged) friend
mi *viejo* amigo—my old (former) friend

*un coche **nuevo***—a (brand) new car
*un **nuevo** coche*—a (different) car

4.5   Determinative Adjectives

Subject	Singular	Plural	
yo	*mi*	*mis*	my
tú	*tu*	*tus*	your
usted	*su*	*sus*	your
él/ella	*su*	*sus*	his/her
nosotros	*nuestro/a*	*nuestros/as*	our
vosotros	*vuestro/a*	*vuestros/as*	your
ustedes	*su*	*sus*	your
ellos/as	*su*	*sus*	their

These adjectival forms **precede** nouns: *mi libro, **tu** pupitre, **su** trabajo, **nuestra** organización.*

Possessive adjectives have modified forms when they follow nouns (for reasons of emphasis) or when they stand alone with the verb "to be." In these cases they must agree in gender and number with the nouns they modify:

Subject	Singular	Plural	
yo	*mío/a*	*míos/as*	my/mine
tú	*tuyo/a*	*tuyos/as*	your/yours
usted	*suyo/a*	*suyos/as*	your/yours
él/ella	*suyo/a*	*suyos/as*	his/her/hers
nosotros	*nuestro/a*	*nuestros/as*	our/ours
vosotros	*vuestro/a*	*vuestros/as*	your/yours
ustedes	*suyo/a*	*suyos/as*	your/yours
ellos/as	*suyo/a*	*suyos/as*	their/theirs

mi libro—**my** book   *mis* libros—**my** books
el libro *mío*—**my** book   *los* libros *míos*—**my** books

nuestra casa—**our** house   *nuestras* casas—**our** houses
la casa *nuestra*—**our** house   *las* casas *nuestras*—**our** houses

- In the case of the third person possessive adjective (*su, sus*), there can be ambiguity in meaning. Spanish often replaces the possessive with the preposition *de* followed by the appropriate pronoun:

su perro	or	*el perro de él*	her dog
		el perro de ella	her dog
		el perro de Ud.	your dog
		el perro de ellos	their (m.) dog
		el perro de ellas	their (f.) dog
		el perro de Uds.	your (pl.) dog

El disco es **suyo** *or* **el** *disco es* **de él, de ella, de Ud., de ellos, de ellas, de Uds.**

4.5.1 Demonstrative Adjectives

They commonly precede nouns*:

	Masculine	Feminine
Singular	*este, ese, aquel*	*esta, esa, aquella*
Plural	*estos, esos, aquellos*	*estas, esas, aquellas*

este edificio—**this** building
estos edificios—**these** buildings
ese día—**that** day
esos días—**those** days
aquellos tiempos—**those** times
aquella idea—**that** idea

- * Placement of the demonstrative after a noun often gives it a negative or pejorative translation:

el chico ese—that so-and-so guy

Note: *Aquel* (in all its forms) shows either physical distance or distance in time.

4.5.2 Interrogative Adjectives

¿Qué? What?
¿Cuál(es)? Which?
¿Cuánto/a? How much?
¿Cuántos/as? How many?

*¿**Qué** hora es?* **What** time is it?
*¿**Cuánto** dinero te queda?* **How much** money do you have left?
*¿**Qué** calle es ésta?* **What** street is this?
*¿De **qué** hotel me hablas?* **Which** hotel do you mean?

Problem Solving Examples:

Q Fill in with the correct forms of the adjectives in parentheses:

Elena es una chica muy _____ (**talkative**) e _____ (**intelligent**). Ella es _____ (**french**), pero su padre y sus dos hermanas _____ (**older**) son _____ (**english**). Este es el _____ (**third**) año que viven en esta ciudad. La suya es una _____ (**great**) familia.

A habladora, inteligente, francesa, mayores, ingleses, tercer, gran. Elena is a very talkative and intelligent girl. She's French but her father and her two older sisters are English. This is the third year that they are living in this city. Hers is a great family.

Habladora is the feminine form of the adjective "talkative" and it agrees with *chica*. The adjective *inteligente* has the same ending for both genders. Adjectives of nationality experience gender and number changes in their endings: *francesa* agrees with *ella* and *ingleses* agrees with both *padre* and *hermanas*. The plural form of *mayor* (older) is *mayores*, which agrees with *hermanas*. The adjective *tercer* is the abbreviated form of the adjective *tercero/a* and it must precede all masculine singular nouns. *Gran* is the shortened form of *grande*; it must be used in front of all singular nouns, both masculine and feminine.

Choose the correct adjectives from the ones provided:

¿(**Qué/Cuál**) día es (**tus/tu**) cumpleaños? Es (**este/esto**) sábado que viene, ¿no? Isabel y Ana aún no te han comprado (**tus/tu**) regalo. Roberto y yo ya te hemos preparado (**nuestros/nuestra**) sorpresa. Está allí, en (**esta/aquella**) caja.

Qué, tu, este, tu, nuestra, aquella.

What day is your birthday? It's next Saturday, right? Isabel and Ana still haven't bought you your gift. Roberto and I have already prepared our surprise for you. It's there, in that box.

When preceding a noun, *qué* (and not *cuál*) must be used. The noun *cumpleaños* has the same ending for both its singular and plural forms; since here it is singular, the adjective *tu* must agree with it. The neuter form *esto* can never be used in front of a masculine noun such as *sábado*. The possessive adjectives *tu* and *nuestra* must agree in gender and number with the nouns they precede. In the last sentence, the word *allí* indicates that the object we are referring to is far from both the speaker and the listener; *aquella* will therefore be the right choice.

Quiz: Adjectives

1. El _____ apartamento que vieron era pequeño y no estaba muy limpio.

   (A) primero   (C) tercero

   (B) primera   (D) primer

2. Sin habernos explicado por qué, el profesor salió dejándonos _____.

   (A) sola   (C) solos

   (B) solo   (D) sorprendido

3. Andando por la calle un día, me di cuenta de que caminar es una de las _____ formas de ejercicio.

   (A) mejores   (C) mejor

   (B) mejoras   (D) mejora

4. Martín sentía una _____ responsabilidad.

   (A) grande   (C) granda

   (B) gran   (D) grand

5. Las zorras eran demasiado _____ para acercarnos.

   (A) feroz   (C) ferozas

   (B) feroces   (D) ferozes

6. La tierra no era muy buena y su padre trabajaba en las _____ condiciones.

    (A) peor   (C) peora

    (B) peores   (D) peoras

7. Querida, ¿no crees que _____ anillo es tan lindo como los otros?

    (A) esto   (C) este

    (B) aquello   (D) esa

8. Mis nietos me regalaron _____ televisor.

    (A) eso   (C) aquel

    (B) esto   (D) esté

9. _____ problemas son fáciles de resolver.

    (A) Estos   (C) Estas

    (B) Estes   (D) Esas

10. ¿_____ es tu número de teléfono?

    (A) Qué   (C) Que

    (B) Cual   (D) Cuál

ANSWER KEY

1.	(D)	6.	(B)
2.	(C)	7.	(C)
3.	(A)	8.	(C)
4.	(B)	9.	(A)
5.	(B)	10.	(D)

CHAPTER 5

Comparison of Adjectives and Adverbs

5.1   Common Adverbs

Adverbs modify verbs, adjectives, and other adverbs and are invariable.

The following is a list of frequently used adverbs:

bien—well
más—more
siempre—always
cerca—near
antes—before
bastante—enough
temprano—early
así—thus, so
entonces—then
todavía—still

mal—badly
menos—less
nunca—never
lejos—far
después*—afterwards
demasiado—too much
tarde—late
casi—almost
luego—later, afterward

*   *Después de* means "after."

Aún is a common adverb whose meaning depends on whether the sentence is affirmative or negative:

Aún quiere trabajar. He **still** wants to work.

Aún no está despierta. She's not **yet** awake.

5.1.1   Adverbs Ending in *-mente*

Many adverbs are derived from the **feminine** forms of adjectives (when such a form is available) plus the addition of *-mente*:

claro/claramente—clearly
rápido/rápidamente—quickly
feliz/felizmente—happily
hábil/hábilmente—skillfully
dulce/dulcemente—sweetly

5.2   Comparison of Equality

This is constructed in the following ways:

Tanto, a, os, as + (noun) + *como*
Tan + (adverb or adjective) + *como*

*Tuve **tantas** deudas **como** el mes pasado.* I had **as many** debts **as** last month.

*Su música es **tan** clara **como** el agua.* Her music is **as** clear **as** water.

*Llegué **tan** tarde **como** ayer.* I arrived **as** late **as** yesterday.

Tanto como (without intervening expressions) means "as much as."

*Tu amigo estudia **tanto como** yo.* Your friend studies **as much as** I [do].

5.3   Comparison of Inequality

The formula for describing levels of superiority is:

más + (noun, adjective, or adverb) + ***que***

*Tengo **más** dinero **que** tú.* I have **more** money **than** you.

*Su auto es **más** caro **que** el mío.* His car is **more** expensive **than** mine.

*Me levanto **más** temprano **que** ella.* I get up earli**er than** she does.

The above formula changes to ***más de*** if a numerical expression is involved and the sentence is in the affirmative:

*Vimos **más de** mil estrellas en el cielo.* We saw **more than** a thousand stars in the sky.

But:

***No** tengo **más que** cinco dólares en el bolsillo.* I have **only** five dollars in my pocket.

Or:

***No** tengo **más de** cinco dólares en el bolsillo.* I don't have **more than** five dollars in my pocket.

The formula for describing levels of inferiority is:

menos + (noun, adjective, or adverb) + ***que***

*Nos dieron **menos** tiempo **que** a ustedes para completar el examen.* They gave us **less** time **than** they gave you to finish the exam.

*Eres **menos** pobre **que** ella.* You are **less** poor **than** she is.

*Tiene **menos** problemas **que** su madre.* She has **fewer** problems **than** her mother.

Just as in comparisons of superiority, the formula for describing inferiority changes to ***menos de*** if a numerical expression is involved. However, unlike comparisons of superiority, even in negative sentences, *de* is used instead of *que*:

*No eran **menos de** cinco los asaltantes.* The assailants were no **fewer than** five.

5.3.1   Special Comparatives

Adjective (Adverb)	Comparative
bueno (bien)—good, well	*mejor*—better
malo (mal)—bad, badly	*peor*—worse
grande—big	*mayor**—older
pequeño—small	*menor**—younger

* *Mayor* and *menor* only refer to age; otherwise, *más (menos) grande (pequeño) que* is used.

*Mi padre es **mayor** que yo; mi hijo es **menor**.* My father is **older** than I; my son is **younger**.

*Esta ciudad es **más grande que** la capital.* This city is **bigger than** the capital.

5.4   Superlatives

In English, the true or relative superlative is rendered by **the most (least) of** a category:

El, la, los, las + *más (menos)* + (adjective) + *de*

*Estos anillos son **los más** caros **de** la tienda.* These rings are **the most** expensive **in** the store.

*Tienes **los ojos más** lindos **del** mundo.* You have **the prettiest** eyes **in** the world.

The special comparatives noted in 5.3.1 are also superlative forms:

El, la, los, las + (special comparatives) + *de*

*Mi hijo es **el mayor de** la clase.* My son is **the oldest in** the class.

5.4.1   Absolute Superlative

Superlatives can also be formed by adding the *-ísimo* ending to adjectives and adverbs. (Some spelling adjustments may be necessary.)

The absolute superlative is usually rendered in English as "very pretty," "very ugly," etc.

lindo/lindísimo—very pretty; *feo/feísimo*—very ugly

tarde/tardísimo—very late; *cerca/cerquísimo**—very near

rico/riquísimo*—very rich; *fácil/facilísimo*(*a*)—very easy

The adjective *malo* has the special superlative *pésimo* in addition to the more informal *malísimo*.

*   Note the spelling changes from "*c*" to "*qu*" in *cerquísimo* and *riquísimo*.

Problem Solving Examples:

Translate and insert the following adverbs:

El lunes llegamos _____ (**early**) a la conferencia. El conferenciante no estaba _____ (**yet**) en la sala. Cuando empezó a hablar, lo hizo _____ y _____ (**sincerely/clearly**). Yo _____ (**really**) pensé que su exposición había sido _____ (**enough**) buena, pero a mi amigo Alfredo le pareció _____ (**too**) larga. Alfredo _____ (**almost**) se fue _____ (**before**) del final.

temprano, aún/todavía, sincera y claramente, realmente, bastante, demasiado, casi, antes.

On Monday we arrived at the lecture early. The lecturer wasn't yet in the room. When he began to speak, he did it sincerely and clearly. I really thought that his statement was good enough, but to my friend Alfred it seemed too long. Alfred almost left before the end.

The equivalent to the English *-ly* is the Spanish ending *-mente*, which must be added to the feminine singular form of an adjective in order to form an adverb (for example: *claramente, realmente*). However, when two adverbs ending in *-mente* are used together, only the last adverb receives the ending *-mente* (*sincera y claramente*).

Complete with the appropriate comparatives and superlatives:

Pedro es _____ (**the oldest**) de sus hermanos. También es _____ (**the nicest**). Su hermano _____ (**younger**) Javier es _____ (**bigger than**) Pedro y es _____ (**the tallest in**) la familia. Javier es _____ (**very handsome**). El habla _____ (**as much as**) Pedro y es _____ (**as nice as**) él pero es _____ (**less interesting**). Pedro tiene _____ (**more than**) treinta años.

el mayor, el más simpático (or el más agradable), menor, más grande que, el más alto de, muy guapo/guapísimo, tanto como, tan simpático como (or tan agradable como), menos interesante, más de.

Pedro is the oldest of his siblings. He's also the nicest. His younger brother Javier is bigger than Pedro and is the tallest in the family. Javier's very handsome. He talks as much as Pedro and is as nice as he but he's less interesting. Pedro is more than thirty years old.

The irregular comparatives *mayor/menor* are generally used to express age, whereas the regular expressions *más grande/más pequeño* can only be used to express size. The addition of *-ísimo/-a* to an adjective or adverb results in an absolute superlative. In front of a numerical expression, the expression *más de* must be used instead of *más que*.

CHAPTER 6

Verbs

6.1 Regular Verbs of the First Conjugation: -*ar* Verbs

The following charts show the indicative, subjunctive, and imperative conjugations of -*ar* verbs using the model *amar* (to love).

6.1.1 Indicative

	Present	Imperfect	Preterite	Future	Conditional
yo	*amo*	*amaba*	*amé*	*amaré*	*amaría*
tú	*amas*	*amabas*	*amaste*	*amar/ás*	*amarías*
él/ella/usted *	*ama*	*amaba*	*amó*	*amará*	*amaría*
nosotros	*amamos*	*amábamos*	*amamos*	*amaremos*	*amaríamos*
vosotros **	*amáis*	*amabais*	*am/asteis*	*amaréis*	*amaríais*
ellos/ellas/ *ustedes* *	*aman*	*amaban*	*amaron*	*amarán*	*amarían*

* The second person pronouns *usted* (abbreviated *Ud.*) and *ustedes* (*Uds.*) consistently take the verbal form of the **third** person singular or plural.

** This pronoun and corresponding forms of the verb are used in Spain only.

6.1.2   Subjunctive

Present	Imperfect		
ame	*amara*	or	*amase*
ames	*amaras*	or	*amases*
ame	*amara*	or	*amase*
amemos	*amáramos*	or	*amásemos*
améis	*amarais*	or	*amaseis*
amen	*amaran*	or	*amasen*

6.1.3   Imperative

There are two types of imperative in Spanish: the formal and the informal. The formal affirmative and negative commands come from the present subjunctive *él* form. The plural will add an -*n*. The informal negative commands also come from the present subjunctive (the *tú* and *vosotros* forms specifically). However, the affirmative singular of the present indicative (unless irregular) comes from the present indicative *él* form, and the affirmative plural is derived from the infinitive (the final -*r* is removed and replaced with -*d*).

Affirmative	Negative
ama (*tú*)	*ames*
ame (*Ud.*)	*ame*
amemos (*nosotros*)	*amemos*
amad (*vosotros*)	*améis*
amen (*Uds.*)	*amen*

One may also express the informal "let's" form of the command by using the *nosotros* form of the present subjunctive.

6.2 Regular Verbs of the Second Conjugation: -er Verbs

The following charts show the indicative, subjunctive, and imperative conjugations of -er verbs using the model *vender* (to sell).

6.2.1 Indicative

	Present	Imperfect	Preterite	Future	Conditional
yo	*vendo*	*vendía*	*vendí*	*venderé*	*vendería*
tú	*vendes*	*vendías*	*vendiste*	*venderás*	*venderías*
él/ella/Ud.	*vende*	*vendía*	*vendió*	*venderá*	*vendería*
nosotros	*vendemos*	*vendíamos*	*vendimos*	*venderemos*	*venderíamos*
vosotros	*vendéis*	*vendíais*	*vendisteis*	*venderéis*	*venderíais*
ellos/ellas/Uds.	*venden*	*vendían*	*vendieron*	*venderán*	*venderían*

6.2.2 Subjunctive

Present	Imperfect		
venda	*vendiera*	or	*vendiese*
vendas	*vendieras*	or	*vendieses*
venda	*vendiera*	or	*vendiese*
vendamos	*vendiéramos*	or	*vendiésemos*
vendáis	*vendierais*	or	*vendieseis*
vendan	*vendieran*	or	*vendiesen*

6.2.3 Imperative

Affirmative	Negative
vende (tú)	*vendas*
venda (Ud.)	*venda*
vendamos (nosotros)	*vendamos*
vended (vosotros)	*vendáis*
vendan (Uds.)	*vendan*

6.3 Regular Verbs of the Third Conjugation: *-ir* Verbs

The following charts show the indicative, subjunctive, and imperative conjugations of *-ir* verbs using the model *partir* (to leave).

6.3.1 Indicative

	Present	Imperfect	Preterite	Future	Conditional
yo	*parto*	*partía*	*partí*	*partiré*	*partiría*
tú	*partes*	*partías*	*partiste*	*partirás*	*partirías*
él/ella/Ud.	*parte*	*partía*	*partió*	*partirá*	*partiría*
nosotros	*partimos*	*partíamos*	*partimos*	*partiremos*	*partiríamos*
vosotros	*partís*	*partíais*	*partisteis*	*partiréis*	*partiríais*
ellos/ellas/Uds.	*parten*	*partían*	*partieron*	*partirán*	*partirían*

6.3.2 Subjunctive

Present	Imperfect		
parta	*partiera*	or	*partiese*
partas	*partieras*	or	*partieses*

parta	partiera	or	partiese
partamos	partiéramos	or	partiésemos
partáis	partierais	or	partieseis
partan	partieran	or	partiesen

6.3.3 Imperative

Affirmative	Negative
parte (tú)	partas
parta (Ud.)	parta
partamos (nosotros)	partamos
partid (vosotros)	partáis
partan (Uds.)	partan

Problem Solving Examples:

Fill in with the correct translations of the regular verbs provided in the parentheses:

Yo _____ (have dinner) con frecuencia en casa de Teresa pero tú nunca _____ (eat) allí. Ayer yo _____ (decided) ir a visitarla. Luis vino conmigo y, entre los dos, le _____ (bought) un ramo de flores. Cuando llegamos, no _____ (there was) nadie en casa. Pensamos que ella _____ (would return) pronto pero no fue así. La próxima vez, la _____ (I will call) por teléfono antes de ir a su casa.

ceno, comes, decidí, compramos, había, volvería/regresaría, llamaré.

I frequently have dinner at Teresa's but you never eat there. Yesterday I decided to go to visit her. Luis came with me and, between the two of us, we bought her a bouquet of flowers. When we arrived, there was no one at home. We thought she'd return soon but it wasn't so. Next time, I'll call her before going to her house.

Ceno and *comes* refer to customary actions and must therefore be in the present tense. The preterites *decidí* and *compramos* refer to completed past actions. *Había* is in the imperfect tense since it describes a state in the past whose completion is not specified. The expression "would return" must be translated into a conditional tense and the expression "shall/will call" is the equivalent of the Spanish future tense.

 Fill in with the correct forms of the verbs provided in the parentheses:

No me (gustar) _____ hacer la tarea. Nunca (comprender) _____ la geometría y las reglas de gramática. Siempre (necesitar) _____ la ayuda de mis padres. Pero ayer, no había nadie en casa para ayudarme. En lugar de estudiar, mi mejor amiga me (visitar) _____ y nosotras (escuchar) _____ música y (comer) _____ palomitas de maíz. Cuando mis padres (regresar) _____, ellos querían ver la tarea. Ellos estaban enojados conmigo. La próxima vez, (hacer) _____ la tarea antes de divertirme.

 gusta, comprendo, necesito, visitó, escuchamos, comimos, regresaron, haré.

I don't like to do homework. I never understand geometry and the rules of grammar. I always need the help of my parents. But yesterday, no one was home to help me. Instead of studying, my best friend visited me and we listened to music and ate popcorn. When my parents returned, they wanted to see the homework. They were angry with me. Next time, I will do my homework before having fun.

Although we say that *me gusta* means "I like" in English, the phrase more approximately means "it pleases me." Since in this case the speaker is talking about the action *hacer la tarea*, *gusta* is in the third person singular tense. *Comprendo* and *necesito* describe actions in the present so they take the present tense. *Visitó, escuchamos, comimos,* and *regresaron* describe events that took place yesterday, so they take the past tense. *Haré* refers to an event that will take place in the future so it is conjugated in the future tense.

Quiz: Comparison of Adjectives and Adverbs–Verbs

1. Juana es muy lista porque ella siempre _____.

    (A) estudio   (C) estudiaría

    (B) estudia   (D) estudiará

2. Juan mide dos metros y Pablo mide un metro y medio. Juan es _____ alto que Pablo.

    (A) tanto   (C) menos

    (B) más   (D) tan

3. Ramón es más guapo _____ Felipe.

    (A) que   (C) de

    (B) como   (D) tan

4. Lo explicaron _____ nosotros.

    (A) menor que   (C) mayor que

    (B) tanto   (D) mejor que

5. María Elena es única. Además de ser bonita, es sumamente amable y atenta. Con razón, todo el mundo dice que es _____.

    (A) simpatiquísima   (C) pesadísima

    (B) loquísima   (D) aburridísima

6. Ninguna de las ventanas está sucia porque la criada las _____ ayer.

    (A) limpio   (C) limpió

    (B) limpiaba   (D) limpian

7. Yo _____ el colegio a los 10 años.

    (A) dejé   (C) dejara

    (B) dejaba   (D) dejase

8. No te _____ en el cuarto de Felipe.

    (A) acueste   (C) acuesten

    (B) acostéis   (D) acuestes

9. Cuando éramos niños, cada día nuestros abuelos nos _____.

    (A) visitaban   (C) visitan

    (B) visitaron   (D) visitamos

10. Sin que yo lo supiera, mi mejor amigo _____ a Alicia al baile el sábado pasado.

    (A) llevo   (C) llevaron

    (B) llevó   (D) lleva

ANSWER KEY

1.	(B)	6.	(C)
2.	(B)	7.	(A)
3.	(A)	8.	(D)
4.	(D)	9.	(A)
5.	(A)	10.	(B)

Irregular Verbs

7.1 Stem Vowel Changes

In the previous chapter, regular verbs were conjugated either by detaching the stem from the infinitive ending (*-ar*, *-er*, or *-ir*) and reattaching it to the appropriate endings for the various persons, tenses, and moods, or by attaching certain endings to the infinitive as a whole (in the case of the future and conditional tenses).

However, many common Spanish verbs are irregular. There are various types of irregularities: the stem vowels and/or consonants may undergo a change, the endings may differ from the regular ones in at least some of the persons, tenses, or moods, or the verb may be thoroughly irregular.

7.1.1 Irregular Present Indicative

a) Verbs irregular in the *yo* form only:

caber	(to fit)	*yo quepo*
caer	(to fall)	*yo caigo*
dar	(to give)	*yo doy*
hacer	(to make/do)	*yo hago*
poner	(to put)	*yo pongo*
saber*	(to know)	*yo sé*

salir	(to leave)	*yo salgo*
traer	(to bring)	*yo traigo*
valer	(to be worth)	*yo valgo*
ver	(to see)	*yo veo*

* Remember that *saber* means to know a fact or how to do something. *Conocer* means to know a person or a place.

b) Verbs irregular in more than one form:

Subject	*decir* (to say/tell)	*estar* (to be)	*haber* (to have–aux.*)
yo	*digo*	*estoy*	*he*
tú	*dices*	*estás*	*has*
él/ella/Ud.	*dice*	*está*	*ha*
nosotros	*decimos*	*estamos*	*hemos*
vosotros	*decís*	*estáis*	*habéis*
ellos/ellas/Uds.	*dicen*	*están*	*han*

Subject	*ir* (to go)	*oír* (to hear)	*ser* (to be)
yo	*voy*	*oigo*	*soy*
tú	*vas*	*oyes*	*eres*
él/ella/Ud.	*va*	*oye*	*es*
nosotros	*vamos*	*oímos*	*somos*
vosotros	*vais*	*oís*	*sois*
ellos/ellas/Uds.	*van*	*oyen*	*son*

*Haber is an auxiliary verb as in: *He hablado contigo.* (I have spoken with you.) The verb *tener* expresses "to have" in a possessive sense as in: *Tengo dos hermanos.* (I have two brothers.) *Tener* can also be used idiomatically: *Tengo que hablar contigo.* (I have to speak with you.) *Tener* means "to have," as in "possess," but *tener* and *que* together mean "to have to do something."

Subject	*tener* (to have)	*venir* (to come)
yo	tengo	vengo
tú	tienes	vienes
él/ella/Ud.	tiene	viene
nosotros	tenemos	venimos
vosotros	tenéis	venís
ellos/ellas/Uds.	tienen	vienen

c)   Verbs with stem changes:

The most common present tense stem changes are: *"e"* to *"ie,"* *"o"* to *"ue,"* and *"e"* to *"i."* The stem will change in all forms except *nosotros/vosotros.*

Subject	*pensar* (to think) *e – ie*	*volver* (to return) *o – ue*	*pedir* (to request) *e – i*
yo	pienso	vuelvo	pido
tú	piensas	vuelves	pides
él/ella/Ud.	piensa	vuelve	pide
nosotros	pensamos	volvemos	pedimos
vosotros	pensáis	volvéis	pedís
ellos/ellas/Uds.	piensan	vuelven	piden

d)   Verbs with spelling changes:

In the present tense certain types of verbs will undergo a spelling change in the **yo** form only to maintain the proper pronunciation.

-cer, -cir = *zco*

conocer	(to know)	yo cono**zco**
traducir	(to translate)	yo tradu**zco**
conducir	(to drive)	yo condu**zco**

-cer, -cir (preceded by a consonant) = **zo**

vencer	(to defeat)	*yo ven**zo***
convencer	(to convince)	*yo conven**zo***

-ger, -gir = j

coger	(to take, to catch)	*yo co**jo***
escoger	(to choose)	*yo esco**jo***
elegir	(to select, to elect)	*yo eli**jo***

-guir = g

distinguir	(to distinguish)	*yo distin**go***
seguir	(to follow)	*yo si**go***
extinguir	(to extinguish)	*yo extin**go***

Verbs ending in **-uir** will have a **"y"** in all forms but *nosotros* and *vosotros*.

huir (to flee): *hu**yo**, hu**yes**, hu**ye**, huimos, huís, hu**yen***

7.1.2 Irregular Preterite Indicative

a) The following verbs share the same irregular endings:

-e, -iste, -o, -imos, -isteis, -ieron

Subject	*andar* (to walk)	*caber* (to fit)	*estar* (to be)
yo	*andu**ve***	*cu**pe***	*estu**ve***
tú	*andu**viste***	*cu**piste***	*estu**viste***
él/ella/Ud.	*andu**vo***	*cu**po***	*estu**vo***
nosotros	*andu**vimos***	*cu**pimos***	*estu**vimos***
vosotros	*andu**visteis***	*cu**pisteis***	*estu**visteis***
ellos/ellas/Uds.	*andu**vieron***	*cu**pieron***	*estu**vieron***

Subject	haber (to have–aux.)	hacer (to make/do)	poder (to be able)
yo	hube	hice	pude
tú	hubiste	hiciste	pudiste
él/ella/Ud.	hubo	hizo	pudo
nosotros	hubimos	hicimos	pudimos
vosotros	hubisteis	hicisteis	pudisteis
ellos/ellas/Uds.	hubieron	hicieron	pudieron

Subject	poner (to put)	querer (to want)	saber (to know)
yo	puse	quise	supe
tú	pusiste	quisiste	supiste
él/ella/Ud.	puso	quiso	supo
nosotros	pusimos	quisimos	supimos
vosotros	pusisteis	quisisteis	supisteis
ellos/ellas/Uds.	pusieron	quisieron	supieron

Subject	tener (to have)	venir (to come)
yo	tuve	vine
tú	tuviste	viniste
él/ella/Ud.	tuvo	vino
nosotros	tuvimos	vinimos
vosotros	tuvisteis	vinisteis
ellos/ellas/Uds.	tuvieron	vinieron

b) Irregular preterites with a -*j*:

Subject	decir (to say/tell)	traer (to bring)	conducir ** (to drive)
yo	dije	traje	conduje
tú	dijiste	trajiste	condujiste
él/ella/Ud.	dijo	trajo	condujo

nosotros	dijimos	trajimos	condujimos
vosotros	dijisteis	trajisteis	condujisteis
ellos/ellas/Uds.	**dijeron***	**trajeron***	**condujeron***

* These differ from the irregular preterite indicatives in chart a, because they end in *"-eron"* instead of *"ieron."*

** All verbs ending in *"-ducir"* have these irregularities.

c) **Ser**, **ir**, and **dar:**

Subject	*ser** (to be)	*ir** (to go)	*dar* (to give)
yo	fui	fui	di
tú	fuiste	fuiste	diste
él/ella/Ud.	fue	fue	dio
nosotros	fuimos	fuimos	dimos
vosotros	fuisteis	fuisteis	disteis
ellos/ellas/Uds.	fueron	fueron	dieron

* *ser* (to be) and *ir* (to go) are identical in this tense.

d) Verbs with stem changes:

In most cases, verbs ending in *-ir* that have a present tense stem change will also have a stem change in the preterite tense. However, the stem changes in the preterite only apply to the third-person singular and plural forms. See the following charts for examples:

Subject	*sentir* (to regret)	*dormir* (to sleep)	*pedir* (to request)
yo	sentí	dormí	pedí
tú	sentiste	dormiste	pediste
él/ella/Ud.	**sintió**	**durmió**	**pidió**
nosotros	sentimos	dormimos	pedimos
vosotros	sentisteis	dormisteis	pedisteis
ellos/ellas/Uds.	**sintieron**	**durmieron**	**pidieron**

e) Verbs with spelling changes:

Verbs ending in *-car*, *-gar*, and *-zar* will undergo a spelling change in the *yo* form of the preterite to maintain the sound of the infinitive.

Subject	*atacar* (to attack)	*entregar* (to deliver)	*rezar* (to pray)
yo	*ataqué*	*entregué*	*recé*
tú	*atacaste*	*entregaste*	*rezaste*
él/ella/Ud.	*atacó*	*entregó*	*rezó*
nosotros	*atacamos*	*entregamos*	*rezamos*
vosotros	*atacasteis*	*entregasteis*	*rezasteis*
ellos/ellas/Uds.	*atacaron*	*entregaron*	*rezaron*

f) Verbs ending in *-uir:*

These verbs will have a "*y*" in the third-person singular and plural forms.

huir   *huí, huiste,* **huyó,** *huimos, huisteis,* **huyeron**
(to flee)

g) Verbs that change "*i*" to "*y*":

Verbs ending in *-er* or *-ir* with two vowels in the stem (*oír* [to hear], *creer* [to believe], *leer* [to read], *caer* [to fall]) will have a "*y*" in the third person singular and plural. These verbs will also have additional accent marks.

caer   *caí, caíste,* **cayó,** *caímos, caísteis,* **cayeron**
(to fall)

7.1.3   Irregular Imperfect Indicative

There are only three irregular verbs in this tense: *ser, ir, ver.*

Subject	*ser* (to be)	*ir* (to go)	*ver* (to see)
yo	*era*	*iba*	*veía*
tú	*eras*	*ibas*	*veías*
él/ella/Ud.	*era*	*iba*	*veía*
nosotros	*éramos*	*íbamos*	*veíamos*
vosotros	*erais*	*ibais*	*veíais*
ellos/ellas/Uds.	*eran*	*iban*	*veían*

Problem Solving Example:

Fill in with the correct conjugations of the irregular verbs provided in the parentheses:

> Me encanta la ciudad de Madrid porque _____ (**estar**) llena de arte. Ayer yo _____ (**ir**) al Museo de Prado donde _____ (**ver**) unas pinturas de Goya. Un guía me _____ (**decir**) que hay belleza por todas partes en Madrid a causa de la pasión por el arte que _____ (**tener**) los españoles.

está, fui, vi, dijo, tienen.

I am enchanted by the city of Madrid because it is full of art. Yesterday I went to the Museo de Prado where I saw some of Goya's paintings. A guide told me that there is beauty everywhere in Madrid because of the passion for art that the Spanish people have.

Fui, vi, and *digo* describe actions that happened yesterday during the speaker's visit to the museum, so they are conjugated in the past tense. *Está* and *tienen* refer to current actions, so they both take the present tense.

7.1.4   Irregular Future and Conditional

These two tenses have the same set of irregular stems to which the normal future and conditional tense endings are added.

caber	(to fit)	*cabr*
decir	(to say/tell)	*dir*
haber	(to have–aux.)	*habr*
hacer	(to make/do)	*har*
poder	(to be able)	*podr*
poner	(to put)	*pondr*
querer	(to want)	*querr*
saber	(to know)	*sabr*
salir	(to leave)	*saldr*
tener	(to have)	*tendr*
valer	(to be worth)	*valdr*
venir	(to come)	*vendr*

7.1.5   Irregular Present Subjunctive

a) Verbs irregular throughout:

Subject	*caber* (to fit)	*caer* (to fall)	*dar* (to give)
yo	*quepa*	*caiga*	*dé*
tú	*quepas*	*caigas*	*des*
él/ella/Ud.	*quepa*	*caiga*	*dé*
nosotros	*quepamos*	*caigamos*	*demos*
vosotros	*quepáis*	*caigáis*	*deis*
ellos/ellas/Uds.	*quepan*	*caigan*	*den*

Subject	*decir* (to say/tell)	*estar* (to be)	*haber* (to have–aux.)
yo	*diga*	*esté*	*haya*
tú	*digas*	*estés*	*hayas*

él/ella/Ud.	diga	esté	haya
nosotros	digamos	estemos	hayamos
vosotros	digáis	estéis	hayáis
ellos/ellas/Uds.	digan	estén	hayan

Subject	*hacer* (to make/do)	*ir* (to go)	*oír* (to hear)
yo	haga	vaya	oiga
tú	hagas	vayas	oigas
él/ella/Ud.	haga	vaya	oiga
nosotros	hagamos	vayamos	oigamos
vosotros	hagáis	vayáis	oigáis
ellos/ellas/Uds.	hagan	vayan	oigan

Subject	*poner* (to put)	*saber* (to know)	*salir* (to go out)
yo	ponga	sepa	salga
tú	pongas	sepas	salgas
él/ella/Ud.	ponga	sepa	salga
nosotros	pongamos	sepamos	salgamos
vosotros	pongáis	sepáis	salgáis
ellos/ellas/Uds.	pongan	sepan	salgan

Subject	*ser* (to be)	*tener* (to have)	*traer* (to bring)
yo	sea	tenga	traiga
tú	seas	tengas	traigas
él/ella/Ud.	sea	tenga	traiga
nosotros	seamos	tengamos	traigamos
vosotros	seáis	tengáis	traigáis
ellos/ellas/Uds.	sean	tengan	traigan

Subject	*valer* (to be worth)	*venir* (to come)	*ver* (to see)
yo	*valga*	*venga*	*vea*
tú	*valgas*	*vengas*	*veas*
él/ella/Ud.	*valga*	*venga*	*vea*
nosotros	*valgamos*	*vengamos*	*veamos*
vosotros	*valgáis*	*vengáis*	*veáis*
ellos/ellas/Uds.	*valgan*	*vengan*	*vean*

b) Verbs with spelling changes:

	-car to *-que* *atacar* (to attack)	*-gar* to *-gue* *entregar* (to deliver)	*-zar* to *-ce* *rezar* (to pray)
yo	*ataque*	*entregue*	*rece*
tú	*ataques*	*entregues*	*reces*
él/ella/Ud.	*ataque*	*entregue*	*rece*
nosotros	*ataquemos*	*entreguemos*	*recemos*
vosotros	*ataquéis*	*entreguéis*	*recéis*
ellos/ellas/Uds.	*ataquen*	*entreguen*	*recen*

	-ger to *-ja* *coger* (to take/catch)	*-gir* to *-ja* *elegir* (to choose)	*-guir* to *-ga* *distinguir* (to distinguish)
yo	*coja*	*elija*	*distinga*
tú	*cojas*	*elijas*	*distingas*
él/ella/Ud.	*coja*	*elija*	*distinga*
nosotros	*cojamos*	*elijamos*	*distingamos*
vosotros	*cojáis*	*elijáis*	*distingáis*
ellos/ellas/Uds.	*cojan*	*elijan*	*distingan*

	-uir to -ya **huir** (to flee)	-cer to -zca or -za **conocer** (to know)	**vencer** (to defeat)
yo	huya	conozca	venza
tú	huyas	conozcas	venzas
él/ella/Ud.	huya	conozca	venza
nosotros	huyamos	conozcamos	venzamos
vosotros	huyáis	conozcáis	venzáis
ellos/ellas/Uds.	huyan	conozcan	venzan

	-cir to -zca **traducir** (to translate)
yo	traduzca
tú	traduzcas
él/ella/Ud.	traduzca
nosotros	traduzcamos
vosotros	traduzcáis
ellos/ellas/Uds.	traduzcan

c) Verbs with stem changes:

If the verb has only one stem change in parentheses, it will occur in all but the *nosotros/vosotros* forms. If there are two stem changes indicated, the first will be found in all but the *nosotros/vosotros* forms and the second will occur in the *nosotros/vosotros* forms.*

	ue **jugar** (to play)	ue, u** **dormir** (to sleep)
yo	juegue	duerma
tú	juegues	duermas
él/ella/Ud.	juegue	duerma
nosotros	juguemos	durmamos

| vosotros | juguéis | durmáis |
| ellos/ellas/Uds. | jueguen | duerman |

* Some verbs have a stem change in the subjunctive. Most of the time the stem change does not occur in the *nosotros/vosotros* forms.

** In some cases (*dormir*) there is a separate stem change in the *nosotros/vosotros* forms.

Problem Solving Example:

Fill in with the correct conjugations of the irregular verbs provided in the parentheses:

Mañana nosotros _____ (**salir**) de Madrid y _____ (**hacer**) un viaje al campo donde _____ (**poder**) saborear la vida rústica. Ojalá que _____ (**hacer**) buen tiempo. Pero, cualquier que _____ (**ser**) el tiempo, vamos a divertirnos. Es importante que _____ (**tener**) un día de descanso.

saldremos, haremos, podremos, haga, sea, tengamos.

Tomorrow we will leave Madrid and we will make a trip to the countryside where we will be able to savor the rustic life. I hope that there will be good weather. But whatever the weather may be, we are going to enjoy ourselves. It is important that we have a day of rest.

This entire paragraph describes events that will (or will not) take place tomorrow. *Saldremos, haremos*, and *podremos* are actions that are certain, so they take the future indicative. *Haga, sea*, and *tengamos* are all in the subjunctive tense because they do not express certainty, and they follow indicators of the subjunctive such as *ojalá, cualquier que*, and the impersonal expression *es importante que*.

7.1.6 Irregular Past Subjunctive

Because this tense is derived from the third person plural of the preterite, it will have the same irregular forms as the preterite. The past subjunctive endings (*-ra* and *-se*) are interchangeable.

a) Irregular throughout:

Subject	*andar* (to walk)	*caber* (to fit)	*dar* (to give)
yo	*anduviera*	*cupiera*	*diera*
tú	*anduvieras*	*cupieras*	*dieras*
él/ella/Ud.	*anduviera*	*cupiera*	*diera*
nosotros	*anduviéramos*	*cupiéramos*	*diéramos*
vosotros	*anduvierais*	*cupierais*	*dierais*
ellos/ellas/Uds.	*anduvieran*	*cupieran*	*dieran*

Subject	*decir* (to say/tell)	*estar* (to be)	*haber* (to have–aux.)
yo	*dijera*	*estuviera*	*hubiera*
tú	*dijeras*	*estuvieras*	*hubieras*
él/ella/Ud.	*dijera*	*estuviera*	*hubiera*
nosotros	*dijéramos*	*estuviéramos*	*hubiéramos*
vosotros	*dijerais*	*estuvierais*	*hubierais*
ellos/ellas/Uds.	*dijeran*	*estuvieran*	*hubieran*

Subject	*hacer* (to make/do)	*ir* (to go)	*poder* (to be able)
yo	*hiciera*	*fuera*	*pudiera*
tú	*hicieras*	*fueras*	*pudieras*
él/ella/Ud.	*hiciera*	*fuera*	*pudiera*
nosotros	*hiciéramos*	*fuéramos*	*pudiéramos*

vosotros	hicierais	fuerais	pudierais
ellos/ellas/Uds.	hicieran	fueran	pudieran

Subject	poner (to put)	querer (to want)	saber (to know)
yo	pusiera	quisiera	supiera
tú	pusieras	quisieras	supieras
él/ella/Ud.	pusiera	quisiera	supiera
nosotros	pusiéramos	quisiéramos	supiéramos
vosotros	pusierais	quisierais	supierais
ellos/ellas/Uds.	pusieran	quisieran	supieran

Subject	ser (to be)	tener (to have)	venir (to come)
yo	fuera	tuviera	viniera
tú	fueras	tuvieras	vinieras
él/ella/Ud.	fuera	tuviera	viniera
nosotros	fuéramos	tuviéramos	viniéramos
vosotros	fuerais	tuvierais	vinierais
ellos/ellas/Uds.	fueran	tuvieran	vinieran

Subject	-ducir* conducir (to drive)	-uir huir (to flee)
yo	condujera	huyera
tú	condujeras	huyeras
él/ella/Ud.	condujera	huyera
nosotros	condujéramos	huyéramos
vosotros	condujerais	huyerais
ellos/ellas/Uds.	condujeran	huyeran

* All verbs ending in -ducir have these irregularities.

b) Verbs with stem changes:

Any *-ir* verb with two stem changes will use the second one through-out the past subjunctive.

> *dormir (ue, u)*   *durmiera, durmieras, durmiera*
> (to sleep)   *durmiéramos, durmierais, durmieran*

c) Verbs with *y*:

All *-uir* verbs, as well as those with double vowels (*oír, creer, leer,* etc.), will have a "**y**" throughout the past subjunctive.

> *huir*   *huyera, huyeras, huyera,*
> (to flee)   *huyéramos, huyerais, huyeran*
> *oír*   *oyera, oyeras, oyera,*
> (to hear)   *oyéramos, oyerais, oyeran*

Problem Solving Example:

Fill in with the correct conjugations of the irregular verbs pro-vided in the parentheses:

> Mis padres siempre querían que yo _____ (**ser**) bien educado. Ellos querían que yo _____ (**poder**) hablar español. Era importante que yo _____ (**saber**) las reglas de la gramática española. Me mandaron que yo _____ (**hacer**) ejercicios cada noche y _____ (**traducir**) libros en español. Hoy en día, estoy contento de que mis padres _____ (**ser**) tan estrictos.

fuera, pudiera, supiera, hiciera, tradujera, fueran.

My parents always wanted me to be well educated. They wanted me to be able to speak Spanish. It was important that I know the rules of Spanish grammar. They made me do exercises every night and translate Spanish books. Nowadays, I am happy that my parents were so strict.

The subjunctive tenses *fuera and pudiera* are used because they follow a form of *querer*, a verb of desire. *Supiera* follows an impersonal expression so the subjunctive is used. *Hiciera* and *tradujera* are used because they follow a command verb, *mandaron*. Likewise, *estoy contento* expresses emotion in the present tense, so the present subjunctive *fueran* is required.

7.1.7   Irregular Imperatives

a)   Irregular formal commands:

Because all forms come from the present subjunctive, they will have the same irregularities. See Sections 7.1.5 a, b, and c for this list. The third person singular and plural are needed.

b)   Irregular familiar commands:

There are nine irregular affirmative singular commands:

decir	(to say/tell)	*dí*
hacer	(to make/do)	*haz*
ir	(to go)	*ve*
poner	(to put)	*pon*
salir	(to leave)	*sal*
ser	(to be)	*sé*
tener	(to have)	*ten*
valer	(to be worth)	*val*
venir	(to come)	*ven*

The affirmative plural commands are derived from the infinitive, which has no irregulars.

Quiz: Irregular Verbs

1. No dudo que _____ un terremoto.

    (A) había   (C) hubiera

    (B) haya   (D) hubo

2. Si _____ dinero, iría a Bolivia.

    (A) tenía   (C) tengo

    (B) tuviera   (D) tuve

3. No estoy segura, pero tal vez, el _____.

    (A) viniera   (C) venga

    (B) vendrá   (D) viene

4. El juez no le creyó aunque _____ la verdad.

    (A) dija   (C) dijera

    (B) dirá   (D) dijo

5. Le pedí que _____ temprano para acabar temprano.

    (A) venga   (C) venir

    (B) viniera   (D) venía

6. No creo que mis amigos me _____ abandonado.

    (A) han   (C) hayan

    (B) habían   (D) hubieran

7. Habla con ella como si la _____ bien.

    (A) conoci   (C) conociera

    (B) conozca   (D) conoció

8. Es evidente que los chicos no _____ en sus cuartos.

    (A) están   (C) son

    (B) estén   (D) seam

9. Mis padres me compraron un auto para que _____ a pasear.

    (A) salgo   (C) salga

    (B) salir   (D) saliera

10. Busco el empleado que _____ escribir bien.

    (A) sabe   (C) supiera

    (B) sepa   (D) supo

ANSWER KEY

1.	(D)	6.	(C)
2.	(B)	7.	(C)
3.	(C)	8.	(A)
4.	(D)	9.	(C)
5.	(B)	10.	(B)

CHAPTER 8

Imperfect vs. Preterite

8.1 Continuation vs. Completion of an Action

The imperfect is used for an action **continuing** in the past; the preterite designates a **finished** action or an action whose beginning, duration, or end is emphasized by the speaker.

> *Estaba nublado.* (Imperfect) It was cloudy. (No indication of when it got that way.)
>
> *Estuvo nublado.* (Preterite) It was cloudy. (But now it has changed.)
>
> *Ella quería a su marido.* (Imperfect) She loved her husband. (Indefinitely in the past.)
>
> *Ella quiso a su marido.* (Preterite) She loved her husband. (While he was alive, while she was married to him, etc.)

8.2 Description vs. Narration

The imperfect is used to **describe** a quality or a state in the past; the preterite is used to **narrate** an action.

> *Los soldados marcharon* (Preterite) *toda una mañana y llegaron* (Preterite) *al fuerte enemigo al mediodía cuando hacía* (Imperfect) *mucho calor. Se sentían* (Imperfect) *cansados y*

necesitaban (Imperfect) *descansar. Se **sentaron*** (Preterite) *a la sombra de un árbol.* The soldiers marched one full morning and arrived at the enemy fort at noon when it was very hot. They were tired and needed to rest. They sat down in the shade of a tree.

8.3 "Used to" Followed by Infinitive

The English expression **used to** followed by an infinitive is rendered by the imperfect, as this is the tense that designates a habitual action in the past.

Pasábamos las vacaciones en la costa. We **used to spend** the holidays on the shore.

Eran amigos. They **used to be** friends.

Alternatively, the verb *soler* (to be in the habit of) may be used in the imperfect to render the sense of "used to." *Soler* must be accompanied by an infinitive: *solíamos pasar las vacaciones en la costa*; *solían ser amigos*, etc.

8.4 "Was" or "Were" Plus Present Participle

Expressions formed with the past tense of "to be" followed by the present participle of another verb (**was** or **were** doing, singing, studying, etc.) are rendered by the imperfect.

*Él **conducía** cuando ocurrió el accidente.* He **was driving** when the accident occurred.

Pensaban visitarnos ese verano. They **were thinking** of visiting us that summer.

8.5 Telling Time in the Past

The imperfect of *ser* is used to tell time in the past.

Eran las tres. **It was** 3 o'clock.

Era tarde cuando se fueron los invitados. **It was** late when the guests left.

8.6   Special Preterites

The preterite of some verbs (such as *conocer, saber, poder, tener,* and *querer*) have special meanings:

*Yo la **conocí** el año pasado.* I **met** her last year.

*Cuando **supimos** la noticia nos pusimos tristes.* When we **learned/found out** the news we felt sad.

*El fugitivo **pudo** abandonar el país a última hora.* The fugitive **managed to** abandon the country at the last minute.

*Ella jamás **tuvo** noticias de su familia.* She never **received** news of her family.

*El ladrón **quiso** abrir la puerta con una barra.* The thief **tried to** open the door with a bar.

*Juan **no quiso** pagar.* Juan **refused** to pay.

Problem Solving Example:

Choose the correct verbal forms:

El sábado pasado mis padres (**viajaban/viajaron**) a Filadelfia. (**Hacía/Hizo**) mucho calor y (**hubo/había**) mucha gente por la calle. Cuando (**llegaron/llegaban**) a casa, (**estuvieron/estaban**) muy cansados.

viajaron, Hacía, había, llegaron, estaban.

Last Saturday my parents traveled to Philadelphia. It was very hot and there were many people along the street. When they arrived home, they were very tired.

Viajaron and *llegaron* both express finished past actions. *Hacía*, *había*, and *estaban* describe states in the past.

Quiz: Imperfect vs. Preterite

1. Al sentarme a la mesa, _____ a mi hermano que me pasara la sal.

    (A) le pidiese   (C) le pedí

    (B) me pedía   (D) le pedía

2. La tierra que su padre trabajaba _____ muy buena.

    (A) no fue   (C) no fui

    (B) no estará   (D) no era

3. Si tuviera más dinero, _____ comprar un coche.

    (A) pudeo   (C) podré

    (B) podería   (D) podría

4. Cuando empezó a llover _____ las ventanas.

    (A) cerraremos   (C) cerramos

    (B) cerrábamos   (D) se cerramos

5. La guerra de Vietnam _____ varios años.

    (A) duraba   (C) duró

    (B) durará   (D) hubo durado

6. Es necesario que _____ con nosotros.

    (A) vas   (C) vayas

    (B) ibas   (D) fueras

7. Cuando era niño, me _____ viendo pasar a la gente por las calles.

    (A) divertí   (C) divertiría

    (B) divertía   (D) divirtiera

8. Mi hija, tengo que ir de compras. Por favor, _____ conmigo.

    (A) vienes   (C) ven

    (B) venga   (D) vengas

9. _____ las nueve de la noche pero no había nadie en casa.

    (A) Fue   (C) Estaban

    (B) Eran   (D) Es

10. Desgraciadamente, no _____ a la nueva profesora de ciencias en la fiesta de anoche.

    (A) sé   (C) supe

    (B) conozco   (D) conocí

ANSWER KEY

1.	(C)	6.	(C)
2.	(D)	7.	(B)
3.	(D)	8.	(C)
4.	(C)	9.	(B)
5.	(C)	10.	(D)

CHAPTER 9

The Subjunctive

9.1 Structure of the Subjunctive

"Subjunctive" comes from a verb meaning "to join beneath." Verbs in the subjunctive mood depend on a main verb to which they are usually joined by *que*.

> *Yo **quiero** que Uds. **vengan** a la fiesta.* I **want** you **to come** to the party.

> *Mi madre **no cree** que el dentista me **tenga** que sacar la muela.* My mother **doesn't think** that the dentist **will have** to extract my tooth.

Note: In the above examples the main clause and the subordinate clause have **different subjects**. The principal use of the subjunctive is after verbs that cause another person to change his/her behavior. Thus, two distinct subjects are usually needed in a subjunctive construction. Compare *Ella quiere salir* (She wants to go out) with *Ella quiere que salga* (She wants [you, him, me] to go out). The subjunctive form (*salga*) indicates that there is a second subject in the sentence, that someone else besides *"ella"* is being asked to go out.

9.2 If/Then Clauses

A special but frequent type of subjunctive construction is the "if/ then" clause, where the verb following "if" is in the imperfect or pluperfect subjunctive and the verb following "then" is in the conditional. This use indicates an unreal or hypothetical situation.

Si ellos me pagaran, yo les haría el trabajo. If they **paid** me, I would do the work for them.

No habría tanto crimen si hubiera menos armas en la calle. There would not be so much crime **if there were** fewer weapons in the streets.

If/then clauses need to be balanced. That is to say that when a compound tense is used in the dependent clause, the independent clause should also have one.

Si me hubieran dado el dinero, les habria pagado. If they **had given** me the money, I **would have paid** them.

Note: In order to emphasize the hypothetical nature of the above situations, it is useful to contrast them with similar sentences in the indicative:

Si me pagan, les hago el trabajo. If they **pay** me, I will do the work for them. (A more immediate possibility than its counterpart above.)

Habrá menos crimen si hay menos armas en la calle. **There will be** less crime if there are fewer weapons in the street. (An affirmation regarding the future, a certainty.)

9.3   Verbs Introduced by *como si* (as if)

Verbs introduced by *como si* will be in the imperfect or the pluperfect subjunctive.

Se sacó la ropa como si tuviera calor. He took off his clothes **as if** he **were** hot.

Ud. había empalidecido como si hubiera visto el diablo. You had become pale **as if** you **had seen** the devil.

9.4 Forms of the Imperfect Subjunctive

The imperfect subjunctive has two different forms, one ending in *-ra* and the other in *-se* (see 6.2.2). They are interchangeable, but the *-ra* ending is more common: *amara* vs. *amase*; *comiera* vs. *comiese*; *partiera* vs. *partiese*, etc.

9.5 Indicative vs. Subjunctive

The **indicative** expresses certainty or factual knowledge. The **subjunctive** does not make direct statements but expresses a range of subjective approaches to a given statement, ranging from an imperative request to doubt and involving emotion, possibility, desire, approval or disapproval, prohibition, denial, etc. From this it follows that main verbs followed by the subjunctive may be divided into various semantic categories according to whether they express commands, denial, emotion, etc. (See below.)

Note: A "fact" in the above paragraph must be construed as something stated as such. The sentence *Dios existe* (God exists) will not be interpreted by everyone as factual, but everyone will interpret it as being stated as a fact by the speaker.

9.5.1 Verbs of Command

Verbs such as *mandar* (to command), *decir* (to tell), *decretar* (to decree), *ordenar* (to order), and *exigir* (to demand) are followed by the subjunctive.

> *Mi padre me **dijo** que me **fuera** de casa.* My father **told** me **to leave** home.

> *El jefe **mandó** que se **trabajara** más.* The boss **commanded** everyone **to work** harder.

9.5.2   Verbs of Request

Verbs such as *pedir* (to ask), *rogar* (to beg), *suplicar* (to plead), and *requerir* (to require) are followed by the subjunctive.

*Le **pedí** que me **diera** dinero.* I **asked** him **to give** me money.

*Me **rogó** que no **fuera** a la India.* She **begged** me not **to go** to India.

9.5.3   Verbs of Proposal

Verbs such as *aconsejar* (to advise) and *sugerir* (to suggest) are followed by the subjunctive.

*Mi padre me **aconsejó** que **fuera** a la universidad.* My father **advised** me **to go** to college.

9.5.4   Verbs of Desire

Verbs such as *querer* (to want), *desear* (to desire), *soñar* (to dream), and *fantasear* (to fantasize) are followed by the subjunctive.

*No **quiero** que **digas** eso.* I don't **want** you **to say** that.

9.5.5   Verbs of Permission

Verbs such as *dejar* (to let, allow) and *permitir* (to permit) are followed by the subjunctive.

*El vecino **dejó** que yo **viviera** en su casa.* The neighbor **let** me **live** in his house.

9.5.6   Verbs of Preference

Verbs such as *preferir* (to prefer) are followed by the subjunctive.

***Prefiero** que no me **vuelvas** a visitarme.* I **prefer** that you not **return** to visit me again.

9.5.7   Verbs of Prohibition

Verbs such as *prohibir* (to prohibit) and *impedir* (to avoid, prevent) are followed by the subjunctive.

*El policía **impidió** que se **consumara** el robo.* The policeman **prevented** the robbery from **taking place**.

9.5.8   Verbs of Emotion

Verbs such as *temer* (to fear), *sentir* (to be sorry), and *esperar* (to hope) are followed by the subjunctive.

***Siento** que no **pudieras** conseguir el puesto.* I **am sorry** you **could** not get the job.

9.5.9   Verbs of Denial and Doubt

Verbs such as *negar* (to deny) and *dudar* (to doubt) are followed by the subjunctive.

***Dudo** que **llueva** hoy.* I **doubt** it **will rain** today.

9.5.10   Verbs of Seeming and Believing

Verbs such as *creer* (to believe) and *parecer* (to seem) are followed by the subjunctive **only** in negative clauses and optionally in interrogative clauses.

***Creo** que la operación **será** exitosa.* I **think** the operation **will be** successful.

***No creo** que la operación **sea** exitosa.* I **don't think** the operation **will be** successful.

9.6   Impersonal Expressions

Some impersonal expressions formed with *ser* + adjective (or noun) implying possibility, doubt, emotion, or necessity take the subjunctive.

Es posible que llueva. **It is possible** that it **will rain.**

Es probable que sea elegido presidente. **It is probable** that **he will be** elected president.

Es importante que paguemos al contado. **It's important** that we **pay** cash.

Ha sido necesario que lo leamos dos veces. **It has been necessary** that we **read** it two times.

9.7   Conjunctive and Adverbial Expressions

Many conjunctive or adverbial expressions require the subjunctive:

para que – in order that
sin que – without
en caso de que – in case that
con tal (de) que – as long as
a menos que – unless
antes (de) que – before

Le compraré una bicicleta a tu hijo para que aprenda (subjunctive) *a manejarla.* I will buy your son a bicycle **so that** he may learn to handle it.

Pasaron meses sin que me llamara (subjunctive). Months went by **without** her calling me.

Avísame en caso de que venga (subjunctive). Let me know **in case** he comes.

Haré cualquier cosa con tal de que vivas (subjunctive) *bien.* I'll do anything **as long as** you live well.

9.8   Temporal Expressions

Certain temporal expressions (also known as adverbial conjunctions) will always prompt a subjunctive:

antes que	(before)
con tal que	(provided that)
sin que	(without)
para que	(so that)
a menos que	(unless)

Ex: **Antes que** *vayas, llamame.*
     Before you go, call me.

Others will require a subjunctive when "futurity" is implied.

hasta que	(until)
cuando	(when)
mientras	(while)
aunque	(although)

Ex: *Estudiaré* **hasta que** *ella llegue.* [futurity]
     I will study **until** she arrives.

But: **Cuando** *hace calor me siento incómodo.* [fact]
      When it is hot I feel uncomfortable.

9.9   Tense Correspondence/Sequence

Setting up the subjunctive clause often requires selecting the present or past subjunctive tense. To determine which to choose, use the verb in the independent clause as the guide. Any verb form associated with the present (present, future, present perfect, command, future perfect) will prompt a present subjunctive in the dependent clause. Likewise any verb form associated with the past (preterite, imperfect, conditional, past perfect, conditional perfect) will prompt a past subjunctive.

Indicative	Subjunctive
yo dudo *yo he dudado* *yo dudaré*	*que cantes*
yo dudaba *yo dudé* *yo dudaría* *yo había dudado* *yo habría dudado*	*que cantaras*

Indicative	Subjunctive
yo dudo *yo dudaré*	*que hayas cantado*
yo dudaba *yo dudé* *yo dudaría* *yo había dudado* *yo habría dudado*	*que hubieras cantado*

Problem Solving Examples:

Choose between the indicative and the subjunctive in the sentences below:

Creo que este apartamento (**es/sea**) más grande que el otro pero dudo que (**tiene/tenga**) más claridad. Tengo miedo de que (**es/sea**) demasiado oscuro. Es verdad que (**tiene/tenga**) bastantes ventanas, pero son todas muy pequeñas. Voy a volver otro día con mi amigo para que me (**puede/pueda**) dar su opinión. No quiero alquilar el piso hasta que (**estoy/esté**) totalmente convencido.

es, tenga, sea, tiene, pueda, esté.

I believe this apartment is bigger than the other one but I doubt that it has more light. I'm afraid it's too dark. It's true that it has enough windows, but they're all very small. I'm going to return another day with my friend so that he can give me his opinion. I don't want to rent the flat until I'm totally convinced.

The affirmative use of *creer* must be followed by an indicative tense. Expressions of doubt (*dudo que*) or emotion (*tengo miedo de que*) require the use of a subjunctive. On the contrary, expressions of certainty such as *es verdad que* must be used with an indicative. The clause *para que* is always followed by a subjunctive. *Hasta que* is used with a subjunctive whenever it refers to a hypothetical future event.

 Fill in with the appropriate conjugated tenses:

Hablas como si _____ (**creer**) que puedo ir a la fiesta. Si _____ (**poder**) ir, no lo dudaría un minuto. De todos modos, quiero que _____ (**llevar**) tú mi regalo. Y te pido que no me _____ (**preguntar**) otra vez si voy a ir o no. Ya sé que sientes que no _____ (**poder**) acompañarte. Si no _____ (**ir**) a la playa el sábado pasado, no me habría resfriado.

 creyeras/creyeses, pudiera/pudiese, lleves, preguntes, pueda, hubiera ido/hubiese ido.

You talk as if you believed I can go to the party. If I could go, I wouldn't doubt it a minute. Anyway, I want you to take my gift. And I want you not to ask again whether I'm going to go or not. I already know that you regret that I can't accompany you. If I hadn't gone to the beach last Saturday, I wouldn't have gotten a cold.

Conditional clauses implying an improbable or impossible condition require the use of the imperfect or pluperfect subjunctive (*creyeras, pudiera, hubiera ido*). Verbs of request such as *quiero que* or *te pido que* and verbs of emotion such as *sientes que* also require a subjunctive.

Quiz: The Subjunctive

1. Si _____ dinero, iría a Bolivia.

   (A) tenía   (C) tengo

   (B) tuviera   (D) tuve

2. Hace seis meses que Marta estudia español, pero lo habla como si _____ mexicana.

   (A) esté   (C) fuera

   (B) sea   (D) estuviera

3. Su madre le dijo que _____ todo o no podría tener postre.

   (A) come   (C) comía

   (B) coma   (D) comiera

4. Le pedí que _____ temprano para acabar temprano.

   (A) venga   (C) venir

   (B) viniera   (D) venía

5. Siento que ellos _____ con Uds. ayer.

   (A) no estuvieron   (C) no estaban

   (B) no estuvieran   (D) no estarán

6. _____ que tienes razón.

   (A) Creo   (C) Niego

   (B) Dudo   (D) Me alegro de

7. La familia Gómez quería visitar México para que los hijos _____ a sus tíos.

    (A) conozcan   (C) conocieran

    (B) conocieron   (D) conocerían

8. Dijeron que nos enviarían el paquete tan pronto como _____.

    (A) lo recibieron   (C) tengan tiempo

    (B) llegara   (D) sabrán nuestra dirección

9. Hijita, ¡no quiero _____ en la calle!

    (A) que juego   (C) que juegas

    (B) que juegues   (D) que jueguas

10. Si _____ a tiempo, habrías visto toda la película.

    (A) hayas llegado   (C) habrías llegado

    (B) hubieras llegado (D) has llegado

ANSWER KEY

1.	(B)	6.	(A)
2.	(C)	7.	(C)
3.	(D)	8.	(B)
4.	(B)	9.	(B)
5.	(B)	10.	(B)

CHAPTER 10

Past and Present Participles

10.1 Formation of the Past Participle

The following charts show the conjugations of regular participles, as well as irregular past participles.

10.1.1 Regular Participles in the First Conjugation

Regular participles in the first conjugation *-ar* end in *-ado*.

Infinitive	Past Participle
amar	*amado*—loved
cantar	*cantado*—sung

10.1.2 Regular Participles in the Second and Third Conjugations

Regular participles in the second and third conjugations *-er* and *-ir* end in *-ido*.

Infinitive	Past Participle
tener	*tenido*—had
venir	*venido*—come

10.1.3 Irregular Past Participles

Some verbs have irregular past participles:

Infinitive	Past Participle
abrir	*abierto*—opened
cubrir	*cubierto*—covered
decir	*dicho*—said
describir	*descrito*—described
descubrir	*descubierto*—discovered
devolver	*devuelto*—returned
escribir	*escrito*—written
hacer	*hecho*—done, made
morir	*muerto*—died, dead
poner	*puesto*—put, set
resolver	*resuelto*—solved, resolved
romper	*roto*—torn, broken
ver	*visto*—seen
volver	*vuelto*—returned

10.2 Uses of the Past Participle

The past participle forms compound tenses with the verb *haber* (to have, auxiliary verb). In this function the past participle is invariable.

*El hombre ha **comido**.* The man has **eaten**.

Past participles, when not accompanied by some form of *haber,* function as adjectives. In these cases they agree in gender and number with the nouns they modify.

*Hay una taza **rota** en la lavadora.* There is a **broken** cup in the dishwasher.

*Mis problemas están **resueltos**.* My problems are **solved**.

10.3 Formation of the Present Participle

Present participles in the first conjugation end in *-ando*.

Infinitive	Present Participle
amar	*amando*—loving
cantar	*cantando*—singing

Present participles in the second and third conjugations end in *-iendo* (*-yendo* when otherwise there would be three vowels in a row).

Infinitive	Present Participle
comer	*comiendo*—eating
partir	*partiendo*—leaving
ir	*yendo*—going
huir	*huyendo*—fleeing

Note: While endings are always regular, some present participles have irregularities in their stems which reproduce those found in the preterite tense.

Infinitive	Present Participle
pedir	*pidiendo*—asking
repetir	*repitiendo*—repeating
morir	*muriendo*—dying
venir	*viniendo*—coming
poder	*pudiendo*—being able to
decir	*diciendo*—saying

10.4 Uses of the Present Participle

The present participle denotes an action in progress and commonly follows the verb *estar.* It corresponds to the "-ing" form of the verb in English. In Spanish it is always invariable.

Los niños están jugando en la plaza. The children are **playing** in the square.

Mañana estaremos tomando el sol en la playa. Tomorrow we'll be **getting** a suntan on the beach.

Note: The present participle never follows the verb *ser.*

Present participles may also follow other verbs, especially verbs of motion such as *ir* (to go), *venir* (to come), *andar* (to go, walk), *entrar* (to enter), *salir* (to go out), etc.

Ella va corriendo por la calle. She is **running** down the street.

Uds. andan contando mentiras. You are **telling** (spreading) lies.

Te vi salir llorando de la entrevista. I saw you leave the interview **crying**.

The progressive tense ("to be" plus a present participle) is not as common in Spanish as in English. It is used only for special emphasis; normally, the simple present is used. Study the following translations:

Ella va a la tienda. She **is going** to the store.

El barco parte mañana. The ship **is leaving** tomorrow.

In English, present participles may function as nouns. In Spanish, this function is taken over by the infinitive.

Fumar es malo para la salud. **Smoking** is bad for your health.

Me gusta bailar. I like **dancing**.

Volar es divertido. **Flying** is fun.

The present participle in Spanish does not follow prepositions.

después de comer—after **eating**

Desde que llegó aquí no para de hablar. Since **arriving** here he hasn't stopped **talking**.

Problem Solving Examples:

Form the correct participle for each sentence:

¿Qué está _____ (**decir**) Marta? ¿Está solamente _____ (**leer**) en alto o me está _____ (**pedir**) algo? No la he _____ (**oír**) bien. Dile que ya he _____ (**ver**) la nota que me había _____ (**escribir**). Dile también que ya he _____ (**resolver**) mi problema y que he _____ (**hacer**) lo que ella me aconsejó.

diciendo, leyendo, pidiendo, oído, visto, escrito, resuelto, hecho.

What is Marta saying? Is she only reading aloud or is she asking me something? I haven't heard her well. Tell her I have already seen the note that she had written me. Tell her also that I have already solved my problem and that I've done what she advised me (to do).

The present participle follows the verb *estar* in order to convey an action in progress. *Diciendo, leyendo,* and *pidiendo* are all irregular present participles. All the other answers require past participles since they are all part of a compound tense. *Visto, escrito, resuelto,* and *hecho* are irregular past participles.

Choose the correct verb forms:

Alfredo entró (**beber/bebiendo**) un refresco y ahora está (**comido/comiendo**) un helado. Después de (**acabar/acabando**) el helado, se comió un pastel. Si sigue (**comiendo/comido**) tanto, va a engordar. Además, (**comiendo/comer**) en exceso no es bueno para la salud.

A bebiendo, comiendo, acabar, comiendo, comer.

Alfred entered drinking a refreshment and now is eating an ice cream. After finishing the ice cream, he ate a pastry. If he keeps on eating so much, he'll get fat. Besides, eating in excess isn't good for one's health.

The present participle can be used with verbs of motion such as *entrar* and also with the verbs *seguir/continuar*. It can never be used after a preposition (*después de*) nor be used as a noun (*comer en exceso...*).

CHAPTER 11

Verbs: Compound Tenses

11.1 Formation of Compound Tenses

Compound tenses are formed by adding an invariable past participle to the different forms of the auxiliary verb *haber* (to have).

11.2 Conjugation of *Haber*: Indicative Mood*

	Present	Imperfect	Future	Conditional
yo	he	había	habré	habría
tú	has	habías	habrás	habrías
él/ella/Ud.	ha	había	habrá	habría
nosotros	hemos	habíamos	habremos	habríamos
vosotros	habéis	habíais	habréis	habríais
ellos/ellas/Uds.	han	habían	habrán	habrían

* The preterite is not conjugated here because it is not commonly used in compound tenses.

11.3 Conjugation of *Haber*: Subjunctive and Imperative Moods

	Present	Imperfect
yo	*haya*	*hubiera/hubiese*
tú	*hayas*	*hubieras/hubieses*
él/ella/Ud.	*haya*	*hubiera/hubiese*
nosotros	*hayamos*	*hubiéramos/hubiésemos*
vosotros	*hayáis*	*hubierais/hubieseis*
ellos/ellas/Uds.	*hayan*	*hubieran/hubiesen*

11.4 Names of Compound Tenses

Compound tenses are formed by combining different tenses of the auxiliary verb (*haber*) with the past participle. The regular past participle in Spanish is formed by appending **-ado** (*-ar* verbs) or **-ido** (*-er* and *-ir* verbs) to the stem of the infinitive.

11.4.1 Perfect

The present indicative of *haber* with a past participle forms the **present perfect** tense:

He amado. I **have** loved.
Han partido. They **have** left.

Note: Only *haber* is conjugated. *Amado* and *partido* do not have to agree in gender and number with their respective subjects.

11.4.2 Pluperfect

The imperfect indicative of *haber* with a past participle forms the **pluperfect** or **past perfect** tense. This tense is used for a past action that precedes another past action:

Había amado. I **had** loved.
Habíais comido. You **had** eaten.
Habían partido. They **had** left.

11.4.3 Future Perfect

The future of *haber* with a past participle forms the **future perfect**:

Habré amado. I **will have** loved.
Habrán partido. They **will have** left.

Note: This tense expresses an action that will take place **before** another. But very commonly the future perfect denotes probability in the past. Compare the following examples:

a) *¿Habrán partido antes de que comience a llover?* **Will** they **have left** before it starts to rain?

b) *Ya habrán partido.* They **probably left** already.

11.4.4 Conditional Perfect

The conditional of *haber* with a past participle forms the **conditional perfect**:

Habría amado. I **would have** loved.
Habrían partido. They **would have** left.

11.4.5 Perfect Subjunctive

The present subjunctive of *haber* with a past participle forms the **present perfect subjunctive**:

*Es increíble que no **haya amado** a nadie en su vida.* It's incredible that he **has** not **loved** anyone in his life.

*Los extrañaremos cuando **hayan partido**.* We'll miss them when they **have left**.

Names of Compound Tenses
87

11.4.6 Pluperfect Subjunctive

The imperfect subjunctive of *haber* with a past participle forms the **pluperfect** or **past perfect subjunctive**:

*Yo no habría conocido la felicidad si no **hubiera amado**.* I would not have known happiness if I **had** not **loved**.

*Él siempre había dudado de que sus amigos **hubieran partido** sin despedirse.* He had always doubted that his friends **had left** without saying good-bye.

Problem Solving Examples:

 Complete with the appropriate compound tenses of the indicative mood:

Si llegas tarde, ellos **ya se** (**habían marchado/habrán marchado**). Teresa (**ha llegado/habría llegado**) esta mañana de San Sebastían. Si hubiese tenido tiempo, te (**he llamado/habría llamado**). Cuando llegó el día de Navidad, los niños ya (**habrán visto/habían visto**) sus regalos.

 habrán marchado, ha llegado, habría llamado, habían visto.

If you arrive late, they will have already left. Teresa has arrived this morning from San Sebastian. If I had had time, I would have called you. When Christmas day arrived, the children had already seen their gifts.

In the first sentence, *habrán marchado* refers to a future action which is previous to the action of *llegar*. The conditional clause in the third sentence indicates an unreal event. In those cases, the conditional tense must be used. Due to tense correspondence with *hubiese tenido*, the conditional perfect has to be used. In the last sentence, *habían visto* refers to a past action that took place before another past action (*llegó*).

Choose the correct compound tenses:

Juan temía que el negocio de su hermana no (**habrá ido/hubiese ido**) bien. No creo que me (**hayan elegido/han elegido**) para este puesto. Si (**había sabido/hubiese sabido**) que ibas a llegar tan tarde, no te (**habría esperado/habré esperado**).

hubiese ido, hayan elegido, hubiese sabido, habría esperado.

Juan was afraid that his sister's business deal had not gone well. I do not believe that they have elected me to this office. If I had known that you were going to arrive so late, I would not have waited for you.

Expressions of emotion (*temía*) or doubt (*no creo que*) require the use of the subjunctive. A conditional sentence referring to an unreal event requires a subjunctive verb in its "if"clause (*hubiese sabido*) and a verb in the conditional tense in its "then"clause (*habría esperado*).

Quiz: Past and Present Participles– Verbs: Compound Tenses

1. Los trabajadores han _____ su labor.

   (A) terminaron   (C) terminados

   (B) terminando   (D) terminado

2. Hace mucho tiempo que yo no _____ con mi mamá.

   (A) he hablado   (C) estaba hablando

   (B) había hablado   (D) hablado

3. Antes del domingo ella _____ el trabajo.

   (A) ha terminado   (C) habrá terminado

   (B) había terminado   (D) habría terminado

4. Depués de que los invitados _____, pidieron el menú.

   (A) han llegado   (C) habrán llegado

   (B) habían llegado   (D) habrían llegado

5. Los niños han _____ tristes desde que sus padres les prohibieron ver televisión.

   (A) sido   (C) estado

   (B) sidos   (D) estados

6. Si yo hubiera sabido la respuesta, se la _____.

   (A) diría   (C) había dicho

   (B) habría dicho   (D) diga

7. Para este viernes ellos _____ la película.

   (A) habían visto   (C) habrán visto

   (B) habrían visto   (D) han visto

8. No creo que mis amigos me _____ abandonado.

   (A) han   (C) hayan

   (B) habían   (D) hubieran

9. Las veinte y una parejas que van a contraer matrimonio esta primavera _____ escogido el mes de abril.

   (A) han   (C) hayan

   (B) habrá   (D) habido

10. Martín _____ allí por los esfuerzos de sus padres.

    (A) llegado   (C) habías llegado

    (B) había llegando   (D) había llegado

ANSWER KEY

1. (D)
2. (A)
3. (C)
4. (B)
5. (C)

6. (B)
7. (C)
8. (C)
9. (A)
10. (D)

CHAPTER 12

The Verb "To Be": Ser or Estar?

12.1 Conjugation of Ser

a) Indicative

	Present	Imperfect	Preterite	Future	Condit.
yo	soy	era	fui	seré	sería
tú	eres	eras	fuiste	serás	serías
él/ella/Ud.	es	era	fue	será	sería
nosotros	somos	éramos	fuimos	seremos	seríamos
vosotros	sois	erais	fuisteis	seréis	seríais
ellos/ellas/Uds.	son	eran	fueron	serán	serían

b) Subjunctive

	Present	Imperfect
yo	sea	fuera/fuese
tú	seas	fueras/fueses
él/ella/Ud.	sea	fuera/fuese
nosotros	seamos	fuéramos/fuésemos
vosotros	seáis	fuerais/fueseis

| *ellos/ellas/Uds.* | *sean* | *fueran/fuesen* |

c) **Imperative**

	Familiar	Formal
	sé (tú)	*sea (Ud.)*
	no seas	*no sea*
	sed (vosotros)	*sean (Uds.)*
	no seáis	*no sean*

d) **Participles**

Past Participle: *sido*
Present Participle: *siendo*

12.2 Conjugation of *Estar*

a) **Indicative**

	Present	Imperfect	Preterite	Future	Condit.
yo	*estoy*	*estaba*	*estuve*	*estaré*	*estaría*
tú	*estás*	*estabas*	*estuviste*	*estarás*	*estarías*
él/ella/Ud.	*está*	*estaba*	*estuvo*	*estará*	*estaría*
nosotros	*estamos*	*estábamos*	*estuvimos*	*estaremos*	*estaríamos*
vosotros	*estáis*	*estabais*	*estuvisteis*	*estaréis*	*estaríais*
ellos/ellas/Uds.	*están*	*estaban*	*estuvieron*	*estarán*	*estarían*

b) **Subjunctive**

	Present	Imperfect
yo	*esté*	*estuviera/estuviese*
tú	*estés*	*estuvieras/estuvieses*
él/ella/Ud.	*esté*	*estuviera/estuviese*
nosotros	*estemos*	*estuviéramos/estuviésemos*
vosotros	*estéis*	*estuvierais/estuvieseis*

ellos/ellas/Uds.	estén	estuvieran/estuviesen

c) **Imperative**

	Familiar	Formal
	está (tú)	*esté (Ud.)*
	no estés	*no esté*
	estad (vosotros)	*estén (Uds.)*
	no estéis	*no estén*

d) **Participles**

Past Participle: *estado*
Present Participle: *estando*

12.3 Uses of *Ser*

"To be" followed by a predicate noun (a noun that is the same person as the subject) is always *ser.*

Él es médico. He **is** a doctor.
Somos hombres con una misión. We **are** men on a mission.

Ser is used to express origin, ownership, or material consistency.

¿Es Ud. de Atlanta? **Are** you from Atlanta?
Ese libro es de la biblioteca. That book **is** the library's.
Esta mesa es de madera. This table **is** (made) of wood.

Ser is used to mean "to take place."

La fiesta fue ayer. The party **was** yesterday.
La reunión es mañana. The meeting **is** tomorrow.

The use of *ser* with an adjective denotes that the speaker considers the quality signified by the adjective an essential or permanent component of the noun.

El agua es clara. Water **is** clear.
La madera es dura. Wood **is** hard.
Mi hermano es alto. My brother **is** tall.

12.4 Uses of *Estar*

Estar is used to indicate location.

El estadio está a dos cuadras. The stadium **is** two blocks away.
Los pañuelos están en el cajón. The handkerchiefs **are** in the drawer.

Estar is used with the present participles of other verbs to form the progressive tense.

Está lloviendo. It **is** raining.
Están comprando los boletos. They **are** buying the tickets.

Estar is used with adjectives to indicate a change from the norm, a temporary state of the subject, or a subjective reaction.

Estaba gordo cuando lo vi. He **was** fat when I saw him.
El postre está rico. The dessert **is** good.

12.5 Adjectives that Change Meaning with *Ser* or *Estar*

Certain adjectives have different meanings depending on whether they are used with *ser* or *estar.*

Mi tío es bueno. My uncle is **good.**
Mi tío está bueno. My uncle is **in good health.**

Tú perro es malo. Your dog is **bad.**
Tú perro está malo. Your dog is **sick.**

La función es aburrida. The show is **boring.**
Mi esposa está aburrida. My wife is **bored.**

Tú eres feliz. You are **fortunate.**
Tú estás feliz. You are **happy.**

Mi hijo es listo. My son is **smart.**
Mi hijo está listo. My son is **ready.**

Este edificio es seguro. This building is **safe.**
El portero está seguro. The porter is **sure.**

Problem Solving Examples:

 Fill in with the appropriate tenses of either *ser* or *estar*:

Ahora Susana _____ segura de que Roberto no _____ su primo.

Ayer por la tarde el niño _____ solo en casa. Espero que no _____ aburrido.

Mi madre no puede ponerse al teléfono porque _____ durmiendo.

 está, es, estuvo, estuviera, estuviese, está.

Now Susana is sure that Roberto isn't her cousin.

Yesterday afternoon the boy was alone at home. I hope he wasn't bored.

My mother can't come to the phone because she's sleeping.

Estar seguro means "to be sure," whereas *ser seguro* means "to be safe." The verb *ser* must be used when referring to permanent attributes such as family relationships (*es su primo*). All expressions of location require the use of *estar* (*estuvo solo en casa*). *Estar aburrido* means "to be bored." *Estar* is used to form the present progressive tense (*está durmiendo*).

 Choose between *ser* and *estar*:

Aunque Patricia no (**es/está**) una mujer demasiado guapa, a mí me parece que hoy ella (**es/está**) muy guapa.

¡Qué bueno (**es/está**) este asado!

La conferencia (**fue/estuvo**) en esta sala.

Ella (**es/está**) dentista pero el próximo año va a (**ser/estar**) dando clases en una universidad.

A   es, está, está, fue, es, estar.

Although Patricia isn't a very pretty woman, it seems to me that today she's very attractive.

How good this roast is!

The lecture was in this room.

She's a dentist but next year she's going to be giving classes at the university.

Ser guapo/-a ("to be good-looking") refers to a permanent quality, whereas *estar guapo/-a* ("to look good") refers to a temporary condition. The second sentence expresses a subjective reaction which is perceived through the senses. "To take place" translates into *ser* and not *estar.* In the last sentence, the verb *ser* indicates the profession and the verb *estar* indicates a temporary state.

Quiz: The Verb "To Be": *Ser* or *Estar*?

1.   No _____ de acuerdo con lo que dicen.

     (A) fui   (C) estamos

     (B) han sido   (D) estuviera

2.   La casa de mi abuelo _____ de cemento.

     (A) ir   (C) está

     (B) es   (D) consiste

3. La boda _____ el 25 del mes entrante.

    (A) estará   (C) fue

    (B) será   (D) estaba

4. ¿De dónde _____ Uds.?

    (A) van   (C) son

    (B) se dirigen   (D) están

5. El padre de Alicia _____ médico.

    (A) está   (C) estaba

    (B) es   (D) estará

6. Los deportistas _____ hombres fuertes y agiles.

    (A) están   (C) son

    (B) hacen   (D) ganan

7. Mi automóvil _____ descompuesto.

    (A) era   (C) está

    (B) es   (D) ha

8. El hotel _____ a cinco cuadras de distancia.

    (A) está   (C) estuvimos

    (B) es   (D) será

9. María _____ más flaca que antes.

    (A) es   (C) está

    (B) come   (D) haría

10. Los deportistas _____ débiles porque no han comido en tres días.

    (A) son   (C) eran

    (B) están   (D) habían sido

ANSWER KEY

1.	(C)		6.	(C)
2.	(B)		7.	(C)
3.	(B)		8.	(A)
4.	(C)		9.	(C)
5.	(B)		10.	(B)

CHAPTER **13**

Classes of Verbs

13.1 Transitive

A transitive verb has both a subject and an object. The latter is called a direct object because the verb acts directly on it. Many verbs in English and Spanish are transitive. In the following examples the transitive verbs and their strict direct objects are in boldface.

*El portero **cierra la puerta**.* The porter **closes** the **door**.
*El pajaro **bebió agua**.* The bird **drank water**.

Note: When the direct object is a person (or a pet), it is preceded by the preposition "*a*," which has no equivalent in English. In Spanish this is called the "Personal *a*."

*Amo **a** mi esposa.* I love my wife.

13.2 Reflexive

A verb whose action reflects back upon the subject is called reflexive. The object of a reflexive verb is a pronoun.

*Mi amigo **se vistió** rápidamente.* My friend **got dressed** (dressed himself) quickly.
*Ella **se miró** en el espejo.* She **looked at herself** in the mirror.

Note: Some verbs are always reflexive while others may be used reflexively. Examples of **reflexive** verbs are: *arrepentirse* (to repent, to be sorry); *atreverse* (to dare); *quejarse* (to complain); *acostarse* (to go to bed); *convertirse* (to become), etc.

13.2.1 Verbs of Becoming

Spanish has several ways to render the idea of becoming. They involve the reflexive verbs *hacerse, ponerse, volverse,* and *convertirse.*

Hacerse implies a conscious effort or an intention of some kind:

Se hará médico cueste lo que cueste. He **will become** a doctor no matter what it takes.

Mi madre se hizo rica por su propia cuenta. My mother **became** rich by dint of her own efforts.

Ponerse implies an unconscious change, physical or emotional:

Te pusiste pálida cuando oíste su nombre. **You became** pale when you heard his name.

Me puse contento al saber la verdad. **I became** happy on learning the truth.

Volverse also implies a change without volition. Also, the "new" state is of longer duration:

¿Te has vuelto loco? Have you **become** (gone) mad?

Mi tío se volvió todo un filántropo. My uncle **became** quite the philanthropist.

Convertirse is basically a synonym for *transformarse* (to transform oneself) and has a physical as well as a moral dimension:

En los cuentos de hadas un príncipe se puede convertir en sapo. In fairy tales a prince may **become** a frog.

13.3 Intransitive

Intransitive verbs denote actions complete in themselves. They have subjects but no objects.

*Los exploradores **durmieron** en la selva.* The explorers **slept** in the jungle.

*El héroe **murió** anoche.* The hero **died** last night.

Note: Some intransitive verbs can be used reflexively. In these cases there is also a change of meaning:

*Ella **irá** mañana.* She **will go** tomorrow.
*Ella **se irá** mañana.* She **will leave** tomorrow.

*El niño **duerme** bien.* The boy **sleeps** well.
*El niño **se duerme** temprano.* The boy **goes to sleep** early.
*El niño ya **se durmió**.* The boy **fell asleep** already.

*Él **parece** sano.* He **appears** healthy.
*Él **se parece** a su abuela.* He **resembles** his grandmother.

13.4 Impersonal

An impersonal verb has an implied subject/object "it." These verbs mostly express nature.

*Siempre **amanece** demasiado temprano.* It always **dawns** too early.
***Anochece** tarde en el trópico.* **It gets dark** late in the tropics.
***Lloverá** mañana.* Tomorrow **it will rain**.
*En Wisconsin **nieva** mucho.* **It snows** a lot in Wisconsin.

Haber is often used impersonally. Only the third person singular is used in this manner.

Hay * *varias personas en la calle.* **There are** several people in the street.

Había *muchas razones para pensar así.* **There were** many reasons to think so.

*   The third person singular of *haber* used impersonally is *hay* and not *ha*.

13.5 Auxiliary

Auxiliary verbs help other verbs express their meanings. The most common auxiliary verbs are *haber* (to have), *ser* (to be), *poder* (to be able to, can, may), *deber* (should, ought to, must), and *querer* (to want).

Haber helps form the compound tenses of verbs:

He visto a Juan. I **have seen** Juan.

Ser forms the passive voice together with a past participle (see 14.1):

El libro fue escrito por Cervantes. The book **was written** by Cervantes.

Poder helps an infinitive express possibility:

Puedo ir mañana a verte. I **can** go tomorrow to see you.

Deber helps an infinitive express obligation:

¡Debes creerme! You **must** believe me!

Querer helps an infinitive express volition:

No quiero verte más. I don't **want** to see you anymore.

Problem Solving Examples:

 Make the correct choices:

Anoche los niños (**durmieron, se durmieron**) muy poco.

No (**se parece, se parece a**) su hermano, aunque son gemelos.

(**Se ha vuelto, Se ha puesto**) muy huraño desde que se murió su esposa.

Juana (**se hizo, se puso**) pálida al oír las noticias.

durmieron, se parece a, se ha vuelto, se puso.

Last night the children slept very litte.

He doesn't resemble his brother, although they are twins.

He has become very shy since his wife died.

Juana became pale upon hearing the news.

Dormir means "to sleep" whereas *dormirse* means "to go to sleep, to fall asleep." *Parecer* means "to seem, to appear" and it is not reflexive. The reflexive *parecerse a* means "to look like, to resemble." *Volverse* implies a longer lasting state than the one expressed by *ponerse*. *Harcerse* implies a conscious effort whereas *ponerse* implies an unconscious, often emotional, change.

Fill in with the missing words:

¿Por qué no traes _____ tu padre contigo?

Why don't you bring your father with you?

Sara no _____ va hasta las siete.

Sara doesn't leave until seven.

Yo no _____ arrepiento de lo que hice.

I don't repent what I did.

Se ha _____ muy contento al oír la noticia.

He became very content upon hearing the news.

Llevó _____ su perro al veterinario.

He took his dog to the vet.

a, se, me, puesto, a.

Traer and *llevar* are transitive verbs which require the presence of an "*a*" whenever the direct object that follows is a person or a pet. The verb *irse* means "to leave" and is used reflexively. *Arrepentirse* is a reflexive verb. *Ponerse* implies an unconscious change of a short duration.

CHAPTER 14

The Passive Voice

14.1 Formation of the Passive Voice

The passive voice is the "mirror image" of the active voice. The object of the active verb (I see **the lion**) becomes the subject of the passive verb (**the lion** is seen by me).

The passive is formed with a form of *ser* and the past participle of a transitive verb. The participle must agree with the subject in gender and number. Compare the following examples:

Active

Los romanos construyeron el anfiteatro. The Romans built the amphitheater.

Passive

*El anfiteatro **fue construido** por los romanos.* The amphitheater **was built** by the Romans.

Note: In this example, there is an expressed agent (by the Romans). However, in many passive sentences the agent is not expressed:

*Las acciones **fueron compradas** a bajo precio.* The stocks **were bought** at a low price.

14.2 Reflexive Substitute for the Passive Voice

It is more idiomatic to replace passive construction by a reflexive construction with the pronoun *se* and the verb in the third person singular or plural. This is especially true of passive sentences that have no expressed agent. Compare with the last example of 14.1:

> *Se compraron las acciones a bajo precio.* The stocks **were bought** at a low price.

Note: As a rule the verb precedes the subject in this type of construction. Other examples:

> *Aquí se habla español.* Spanish **is spoken** here.

> *Se establecieron nuevas reglas para el juego.* New rules **were established** for the game.

14.3 Third Person Plural Active Equivalents for the Passive Voice

It is common, especially in conversation, to use an active construction in the third person plural to render the meaning of passive constructions like the ones in 14.2. In these cases the subject is vague (they, people, someone, etc.).

> *Compraron las acciones a bajo precio.* **They bought** the stocks at a low price.

> *Aquí hablan español.* **They speak** Spanish here.

> *Establecieron nuevas reglas para el juego.* **They established** new rules for the game.

14.4 Impersonal Substitute

The examples given in 14.2 and 14.3 use both the third person singular and the third person plural depending on the number of the subject. But some passive substitutes allow only the third person singular even when the subject is plural.

Se elogió a María. Maria **was praised**.

In this example the *se* may be viewed as equivalent to the English impersonal subject "one." Consequently, the verb following it must be in the singular form.

14.5   The Past Participle of *Morir*

Although "to kill" is *matar* in Spanish and "to die" is *morir,* the form used in passive constructions to render the idea of "having been killed" is the past participle of *morir, muerto.*

*Los manifestantes **fueron muertos** a balazos.* The demonstrators **were shot to death**.

14.6   The Apparent Passive: *Estar* Plus the Past Participle

The true passive in Spanish is formed with *ser* and a past participle (see 14.1). Constructions formed with *estar* and a past participle are different. Instead of expressing an action carried out by an explicit or implicit agent, the apparent passive denotes a state or a condition resulting from a previous action. The past participle becomes an adjective. Compare the following examples:

Apparent Passive
*La puerta **está** abierta.* The door **is** open. (The action of opening it happened earlier.)

True Passive
*La puerta **es** abierta por el niño.* The door **is opened** by the boy. (We see the action happening now.)

Apparent Passive
*La pieza **estaba** reservada.* The room **was** reserved. (Someone reserved it earlier.)

True Passive

*La pieza había **sido reservada** por el turista.* The room had **been reserved** by the tourist.

Problem Solving Example:

Underline all examples of passive voice in the paragraph below:

> El edificio se construyó en el siglo XVIII. Se contrató a varios arquitectos en el extranjero. Los dueños originales vendieron la casa al ayuntamiento y ésta fue ocupada más tarde por la Secretaria de Asuntos Sociales. A principios del siglo el edificio estaba ya muy viejo y fue abandonado. Finalmente, la casa se derrumbó.

se construyó, se contrató, fue ocupada, fue abandonado, se derrumbó.

The building <u>was built</u> in the 18th century. Several architects <u>were contracted</u> from outside the country. The original owners sold the house to the municipal government and the latter <u>was occupied</u> later by the Secretary of Social Affairs. At the beginning of the century, the building was already very old and <u>was abandoned</u>. Finally, the house <u>was demolished</u>.

Se construyó is a reflexive substitute for the passive voice and *se contrató* is an impersonal substitute for it. *Fue ocupada* and *fue abandonado* are common examples of passive voice. *Derrumbarse* is a reflexive verb meaning "to collapse," but if the intended meaning is "was demolished" then it is not reflexive and should be considered an example of a passive construction.

CHAPTER 15

Time and Weather Expressions

15.1 Measures of Time

The word *tiempo* in Spanish designates both "time" and "weather," as in the following examples:

*Ha pasado tanto **tiempo** desde que nos vimos.* So much **time** has passed since we saw each other.

*¿Qué **tiempo** hace hoy?* How is the **weather** today?

The following are some of the expressions Spanish uses to measure or divide time.

15.1.1 Seasons of the Year

las estaciones—the seasons
el verano—summer
el invierno—winter

el otoño—fall
la primavera—spring

15.1.2 Months of the Year

el mes—the month
enero—January   *febrero*—February
marzo—March   *abril*—April
mayo—May   *junio*—June
julio—July   *agosto*—August
septiembre—September   *octubre*—October
noviembre—November   *diciembre*—December

Note: In Spanish the names of the months are not capitalized.

15.1.3 Days of the Week

el día—the day   *la semana*—the week
el lunes—Monday   *el martes*—Tuesday
el miércoles—Wednesday   *el jueves*—Thursday
el viernes—Friday   *el sábado*—Saturday
el domingo—Sunday

Note: The days of the week (which are not capitalized in Spanish) are preceded by the definite article except after a form of *ser*:
el lunes—Monday, on Monday; *los lunes*—Mondays, on Mondays; *es lunes*—it is Monday

15.1.4 Other Expressions of Time

hoy—today   *ayer*—yesterday
mañana—tomorrow*   *anoche*—last night
anteanoche—the night   *anteayer*—the day before
   before last   yesterday
pasado mañana—the day   *el día siguiente*—the following
   after tomorrow   day
la madrugada—dawn   *la mañana*—the morning*
el mediodía—noon   *la tarde*—afternoon
la noche—night (time)   *la medianoche*—midnight

*   Be sure to distinguish between *mañana* (tomorrow) and *la mañana* (the morning).

15.2 Telling Time

When telling the time of day the word "time" is rendered as *hora*.

*¿Qué **hora** es?* What **time** is it?

When telling the hours of the day Spanish uses the feminine definite article before the time expression.

*Es **la** una.* It's one o'clock.

*Son **las** dos.* It's two o'clock.

Note: To specify A.M. or P.M., Spanish uses *de la mañana* and *de la tarde,* respectively.

*Son las tres **de la mañana**.* It's three A.M.

*Son las cinco **de la tarde**.* It's five P.M.

To render the half-hour Spanish uses *media.* To render the quarter-hour, *cuarto* or *quince* are used.

*Son las diez y **cuarto**. Son las diez y **quince**.* It's a **quarter** past ten. It's 10:**15**.

*Son las diez y **media**.* It's 10:**30**. It's **half past** ten.

*Son las once menos **cuarto**. Son las once menos **quince**.* It's a **quarter** of eleven.

Falta un **cuarto** (Faltan **quince**) para las once.* It's a **quarter** of eleven.

*   *Faltar* means "to be wanting, lacking."

Note: *y* is used through the half-hour and ***menos*** is used after the half-hour.

Portions of time other than the half- or quarter-hour are expressed thus:

Son las seis y diez. It's 6:10.

Son las seis y veinte. It's 6:20.

Son las siete menos veinte. It's 6:40. (*Faltan veinte para las siete.*) (It's twenty of seven.)

15.3 *Hacer* with Expressions of Time

With expressions of time *hacer* (to make) is an impersonal verb. Only the third person singular is used.

15.3.1 *Hace (Tiempo) Que* + Present Indicative of Main Verb

This formula shows that the action is still going on in the present. Note that Spanish uses the simple present where English uses the present perfect.

Hace una semana que los equipos no juegan.

The teams have not played for a week.

Hace muchos días que llueve.

It has been raining for many days.

Note: By turning the sentence around, the conjunction *que* can be suppressed. (In negative sentences it is possible to use the perfect tense.)

Los equipos no juegan hace una semana. (*Los equipos no han jugado hace una semana*).

The teams have not played for a week.

Llueve hace muchos días.

It has been raining for many days.

15.3.2 *Hace (Tiempo) Que* + Preterite of Main Verb

This formula designates the sense of time expressed by the English particle "ago."

Hace tres días que la vi. (*La vi hace tres días.*)

I saw her three days ago.

Hace años que nos dejaron. (Nos dejaron hace años.)

They left us years ago.

15.3.3 *Hacía (Tiempo) Que* + Imperfect of Main Verb

This formula shows that the action was still going on in the past.

Hacía tres días que llovía. (Llovía hacía tres días.)

It had been raining for three days.

Hacía tiempo que te esperaba. (Te esperaba hacía tiempo.)

I had been waiting for you for a while.

15.4 Age

Cumplir años and *Tener años* are the expressions most commonly used to indicate age:

Mi padre tiene cuarenta y dos años.

My father is forty-two (years of age).

Hoy es mi cumpleaños. Cumplo ocho.

Today is my birthday. I turn eight.

15.5 Weather Expressions

In English these weather expressions are formed with the verb "to be"; in Spanish they are formed with the verb *hacer* used impersonally.

Hace *calor.* It **is** hot.

Hizo *frío.* It **was** cold.

Hará *buen tiempo.* The weather **will be** good.

Hace *sol.* It **is** sunny.

Hacía *viento.* It **was** windy.

*¿Qué tiempo **hace**?* What **is** the weather (like)?

Hace *mal tiempo.* The weather **is** bad.

15.5.1 With *Tener*

When the sentence is personal, Spanish uses *tener* where English uses "to be."

Tengo *calor.* I **am** hot.
Teníamos *frío.* We **were** cold.

15.5.2 With *Haber* Used Impersonally

Notice that the third-person singular of the present indicative changes from *ha* to *hay* when *haber* is impersonal. *Haber* is commonly used with weather conditions that are visible (*viento, sol, neblina,* etc.).

Hay *neblina.* It **is** misty (foggy).
Hubo *humedad.* It **was** damp.
Habrá *tempestad.* It **will be** stormy.

15.5.3 With *Nevar* and *Llover*

"To snow" and "to rain" are rendered by the impersonal verbs *nevar* and *llover,* respectively:

*Ayer **nevó**.* **It snowed** yesterday.
*Mañana **lloverá**.* Tomorrow **it will rain**.

Problem Solving Examples:

Complete with the appropriate words:

¿Cuánto _____ hace _____ no ves a Mónica? Yo la vi _____ dos semanas, _____ sábado pasado a _____ seis _____ la tarde. _____ varios meses que no la veía. Al _____ siguiente fuimos a celebrar su cumpleaños. Mónica _____ ahora veintitrés años.

 tiempo, que, hace, el, las, de, Hacía, día, tiene.

How long has it been that you haven't seen Monica? I saw her two weeks ago, last Saturday at 6:00 P.M. I hadn't seen her for several months. On the following day we went to celebrate her birthday. Monica is now 23.

¿Cuanto tiempo hace que _____? is used to ask how long something has been going on. If the same structure is used with the verb in the preterite tense, as in the answer *Yo la vi hace dos semanas,* it will then mean how long ago something happened. A similar construction can also be found with both the verb *hacer* and the other verb in the imperfect tense (*Hacía varios meses que no la veía*) and it means how long something had been going on in the past. The translation for "on Saturday" is *el sábado.* The feminine article *la-las* must be used when telling the hours of the day. To render the meaning of "P.M.," the Spanish language uses *de la tarde.* The verb *tener* is necessary in Spanish in order to express age.

 Fill in the blanks:

¿Qué _____ hace hoy? Ayer _____ la noche la radio anunció que iba a _____ calor y que iba a _____ bastante humedad. Es verdad que ahora _____ sol pero yo no _____ calor sino un poco de frío.

 tiempo, por, hacer, haber, hace, tengo.

What's the weather like today? Yesterday evening the radio announced that is was going to be hot and that it was going to be quite humid. It's true that now it's sunny but I'm not warm but a bit cold.

The first sentence asks about the weather and requires the noun *tiempo. Por la noche* means "at night." The verb *hacer* is used with *sol* and with *calor.* The verb *haber* is used with other expressions such as *humedad.* Spanish uses *tener* to express the meaning of "to be hot/cold."

Quiz: Classes of Verbs, Passive Voice, and Time and Weather

1. ¿Cuanto tiempo _____ que andas sin coche?

    (A) hacía   (C) hizo

    (B) haces   (D) hace

2. _____ muchas revistas en la biblioteca.

    (A) Están   (C) Son

    (B) Hay   (D) Han

3. Hacía dos horas que ellos _____ cuando alguien tocó a la puerta.

    (A) charlaron   (C) habían charlado

    (B) charlan   (D) charlaban

4. ¿Cuánto tiempo hacía que _____ cuando entraron?

    (A) hablaban   (C) han hablado

    (B) habían hablado   (D) hablan

5. ¿Cuántos años _____ Juana ahora?

    (A) es   (C) tiene

    (B) está   (D) ha

6. Mañana _____ buen tiempo, según el pronóstico.

    (A) será   (C) tendrá

    (B) estará   (D) hará

7. Es un buen día hoy; hace _____.

    (A) muy calor   (C) mucho calor

    (B) mucho caluroso   (D) muy caloroso

8. _____ tres horas que regresó de su viaje.

    (A) Hacen   (C) Hace

    (B) Ha   (D) Desde

9. _____ lunes pasado, cuando recibieron la llamada, decidieron ir a Rosario de inmediato.

    (A) El   (C) Un

    (B) En   (D) Los

10. El sábado pasado Elvis durmió hasta las diez _____.

    (A) en la noche   (C) en la mañana

    (B) por la mañana   (D) de la mañana

ANSWER KEY

1.	(D)	6.	(D)
2.	(B)	7.	(C)
3.	(D)	8.	(C)
4.	(A)	9.	(A)
5.	(C)	10.	(D)

CHAPTER 16

Personal Pronouns

16.1 Personal Pronoun Chart

Pronouns

Subject Pronouns	Direct Object Pronouns	Indirect Object Pronouns	Reflexive Pronouns	Prepositional Pronouns
yo	me	me	me/mí	mí
tú	te	te	te/ti	ti
él	lo *	le	se/sí	él
ella	la	le	se/sí	ella
ello	lo	le	se/sí	ello
Ud.	lo (la)	le	se/sí	Ud.
nosotros	nos	nos	nos/nosotros	nosotros
vosotros	os	os	os/vosotros	vosotros
ellos	los*	les	se/sí	ellos
ellas	las	les	se/sí	ellas
Uds.	los (las)	les	se/sí	Uds.

* In Spain the direct object pronouns *lo* and *los* are usually replaced by *le* and *les* when the pronoun relates to a person or to a thing personified. The present book observes the Latin American usage throughout.

16.2 Subject Pronouns

These pronouns are usually omitted in Spanish as the verbal form by itself indicates person and number. (For the sake of clarity, *Ud.* and *Uds.* are usually not omitted.) Naturally subject pronouns are used when confusion would otherwise result and in order to emphasize a statement. Often the particle *mismo* (*misma, mismos, mismas*) is used to add emphasis.

> *Fue a comprar vino.* **He went** to buy wine.
> *Ud. fue a comprar vino.* **You went** to buy wine.
> *Ud. mismo fue a comprar vino.* **You yourself went** to buy wine.

16.2.1 Second Person Subject Pronouns

Tú (you, sing.) differs from *usted* in terms of familiarity. *Tú* is more intimate; *usted* more formal. As a rule of thumb, *tú* is used with those people with whom the speaker is on a first-name basis.

In certain parts of Latin America (Argentina, Uruguay, Paraguay, Central America), the form *vos* is often used instead of *tú*.

Vos comes with its own verbal forms: *Vos venís a la hora que querés* (*Tú vienes a la hora que quieres*). You come at whatever time it pleases you.

Vosotros (you, pl.) differs from *ustedes* regionally. In Latin America and in southern Spain *vosotros* has been replaced by *ustedes*.

16.2.2 *Ser* Followed by a Subject Pronoun

In Spanish, the subject pronoun follows "to be."

Soy yo. It is **I**.

*Fue **ella** quien me envió el regalo.* It was **she** who sent me the present.

16.3 Object Pronouns

The direct object pronouns answer the question "whom" or "what"; the indirect object pronouns answer the question "to (for) whom" or "to (for) what."

*Nosotros **lo** vimos.* We saw **him**. (**Whom** did we see?)

*Ella **me** dio un regalo.* She gave **me** a present. (**To whom** did she give a present?)

16.3.1 Prepositional Complement with Indirect Object Pronoun

The indirect object pronoun can be clarified or emphasized by the addition of a prepositional complement (*a* + prepositional pronoun).

*Yo **le** hablé ayer.* Yesterday I spoke to **him/her/you**.
*Yo **le** hablé **a ella** ayer.* Yesterday I spoke to **her**.

16.3.2 Special Uses of the Indirect Object Pronoun

a) **Redundant Indirect Object Pronoun.** An indirect object pronoun is used in Spanish even when the indirect object noun is present in the sentence. The latter, however, must designate a person.

*__Les__ dije a **los empleados** que trabajaran más.* I told **the employees** to work harder.

b) **Dative of Interest.** Indirect object pronouns are also used to represent the interested party involved in the action designated by the verb. (In these cases English uses a possessive adjective or pronoun.) These are usually expressed with FROM + PERSON in English.

__Me__ robaron la billetera. They stole **my** wallet **from me**.

*Ella siempre **le** esconde la medicina **al paciente**.* She always hides the medicine **from the patient**.

16.3.3 Special Uses of the Direct Object Pronoun

a) **Neuter Direct Object Pronoun**. In English, the verb "to be" does not require a direct object pronoun, but in some cases both *estar* and *ser* need a **neuter** direct object pronoun. When a question with a form of *ser* or *estar* is followed by an adjective or noun, the neuter object pronoun *lo* replaces that adjective or noun in the reply. In these cases *lo* refers back to the whole idea expressed in the previous sentence.

¿Es Ud. médico? Sí, lo soy. Are you a doctor? Yes, I am.

¿Estáis enfermos? No, no lo estamos. Are you sick? No, we are not.

Lo is also used with *saber* and *creer* when referring to an event, happening, or thought.

¿Sabes que Catalina se casó ayer? Sí, lo sé. Do you know that Catalina got married yesterday? Yes, I know.

¿Tienes dinero que prestarme? ¡Ya lo creo! Do you have money to lend me? You bet!

b) ***Haber* with Direct Object Pronoun**. The verb *haber* sometimes requires the use of a direct object pronoun unknown in English. Note that the direct object pronoun in the following example is no longer neuter.

¿Hay chicas en la fiesta? Sí, las hay. Are there girls at the party? Yes, there are.

c) ***Todo* with Direct Object Pronoun**. A direct object pronoun is required before the verb when the object of the verb is *todo*. Note that the object pronoun agrees in number and gender with *todo*.

Lo he visto todo. I have seen everything.

Las aprendí todas. I learned them all.

16.3.4 Position of Object Pronouns in the Sentence

Unlike those in English, object pronouns in Spanish precede verbs (see examples in 16.3.3). However, they are attached at the end of the verb when the verbal form is an affirmative command, an infinitive, or a present participle.

> *Ud. **le** escribe.* You write **to him**.
> *¡Escríbale!* Write **to him**!

> *Uds. **la** perdonaron.* You forgave **her**.
> *Hubo que perdonarla.* It was necessary to forgive **her**.

> ***Los** dejó sobre la mesa.* He left **them** on the table.
> *Salió dejándolos sobre la mesa.* He went out leaving **them** on the table.

Note: When the infinitive or the present participle is subordinated to an auxiliary verb such as *querer, ir, poder,* or *estar,* the direct object pronoun can go at the beginning of the sentence or at the end, attached to the infinitive or present participle:

> *Voy a verlo.* I'm going to see **him**.
> ***Lo** voy a ver.* I'm going to see **him**.

> ***La** estoy mirando.* I'm looking at **her**.
> *Estoy mirándola.* I'm looking at **her**.

16.3.5 Syntactic Order of Object Pronouns

When a verb has two object pronouns, the indirect object pronoun precedes the direct object pronoun.

> *Envían una carta.* They send a letter.
> ***Nos** envían una carta.* They send a letter **to us**.
> ***Nos la** envían.* They send **it to us**.
> *¡Envíenosla!* Send **it to us**!
> *¡No **nos la** envíen!* Don't send **it to us**!

But when the two object pronouns in the sentence are third person pronouns, the **indirect** object pronoun (*le* or *les*) is replaced by *se*.

Escribes una carta. You write a letter.
Les *escribes una carta.* You write a letter **to them**.
Se la escribes. You write **it to them**.
¡Escríbesela! Write **it to them**!

16.4 Reflexive Pronouns

The use of reflexive pronouns is to designate actions which the subject does to him/herself. English uses pronouns such as myself, herself, themselves, etc., to designate reflexive actions. Study the following examples:

Lavo los platos. I wash the dishes.

Me *lavo.* I wash **myself**.

Me ves detrás de ti en el espejo. You see me behind you in the mirror.

Te *ves en el espejo.* You see **yourself** in the mirror.

Note: Some verbs are inherently reflexive:

Ella se arrepiente de sus errores. She **repents** for her errors.

16.4.1 Reflexive Pronouns as Prepositional Objects

When a reflexive pronoun follows a preposition, its form changes to *mí, ti, sí,* etc. Compare:

Ud. le habrá dicho a ella que no. You probably said no **to her**. (indirect object pronoun with prepositional complement)

Ud. se habrá dicho a sí mismo que no. You probably said no **to yourself**. (reflexive pronoun with prepositional complement)

La actriz vio su rostro en el espejo. The actress saw her face in the mirror.

La actriz se vio a sí misma en el espejo. The actress saw **herself** in the mirror.

Note: When *mí, ti,* and *sí* are governed by the preposition *con,* both participles are joined to form *conmigo, contigo,* and *consigo.*

Ella fue conmigo al estadio. She went to the stadium **with me.**

Yo quería estar contigo. I wanted to be **with you.**

Los ladrones se llevaron las joyas consigo. The thieves took the jewels away **with them.**

16.4.2 Reciprocal Actions

A reciprocal action is a reflexive action involving more than one subject. It is commonly translated as "each other." In reciprocal constructions the verb is always in the plural.

Cuando Juan y Laura se encontraron, se contaron muchas anécdotas. When Juan and Laura **met each other**, they **told one another** many anecdotes.

Note: Often it is hard to say whether the action in question is reflexive or reciprocal:

Los hermanos Serrano se odian. The Serrano brothers **hate themselves**. The Serrano brothers **hate each other**.

But Spanish has ways to make a clear distinction between reflexive and reciprocal sentences:

Los hermanos Serrano se odian el uno al otro. The Serrano brothers hate **each other**.

Nos engañamos a nosotros mismos con esa ilusión. We deceive **ourselves** with that illusion.

Nos engañamos el uno al otro con esa ilusión. We deceive **each other** with that illusion.

16.4.3 Syntactic Order of Reflexive Pronouns

A reflexive pronoun always precedes either an indirect or a direct object pronoun.

> *Tomó la sopa con gusto.* He enjoyed the soup.
> *Se tomó la sopa con gusto.* He enjoyed the soup.*
> *Se la tomó con gusto.* He enjoyed **it**.

* Reflexive pronouns can be used with some verbs to make the action more personal. *Se comió el postre* (he ate the dessert) is more idiomatic than *comió el postre.*

16.4.4 Reflexive Pronouns and Accident vs. Purpose

In the following examples the use of a reflexive pronoun preceding an indirect object pronoun attenuates the degree of causality or purpose involved in the action. In other words, the action occurs accidentally or unexpectedly. The verb may be singular or plural.

> *Se me cayó el plato.* I dropped the plate (the plate fell down **on me**).

> *Se le escapó el prisionero.* His prisoner escaped (**on him**).

> *Se nos perdieron las cartas.* We lost the letters (the letters got lost **on us**).

> *Se les rompió el vidrio.* They broke the glass (the glass went and broke **on them**).

16.5 Prepositional Pronouns

The prepositions *entre* (between) and *según* (according to) **do not** take the expected pronouns but take instead the subject pronouns.

> *Entre tú y yo, no me gusta nada el profesor.* Between **you** and **me**, I don't like the teacher at all.

> *El presidente se equivocó, según tú.* The president made a mistake, according to **you**.

Problem Solving Examples:

 Complete with the correct personal pronouns:

Lo hice _____ mismo.

I did it myself.

Tú les dijiste a _____ que no vinieran.

You told them not to come.

Ellos ya _____ tienen todo.

They already have it all.

Ramón sólo piensa en _____ mismo.

Ramón only thinks about himself.

Dime: ¿quién, según _____, ganará las elecciones?

Tell me: who, according to you, will win the election?

Los dos vecinos se cortan el pelo el _____ al otro.

Both neighbors cut each other's hair.

 yo, ellos/ellas, lo, sí, tú, uno.

The first sentence needs a subject pronoun. The second one requires a redundant prepositional pronoun that agrees with the indirect object pronoun *les*. When *todo* is used as a direct object in a sentence, a direct object pronoun agreeing with *todo* must also be used. The third person reflexive pronoun to be used after a preposition is "*sí*." After *según*, the subject form of the pronoun is used. *El uno al otro* is used sometimes to distinguish a reciprocal construction from a reflexive one.

 Indicate the position(s) that each pronoun in parentheses could occupy in the sentence that precedes it:

Ya expliqué lo que tiene que hacer (**le/ella**).

I already explained what she has to do.

No he comprado nada (**me**).

I have not bought anything for me.

Creo que voy a avisar ahora mismo (**las**).

I think I'm going to advise them right now.

Es mejor que no la mandes (**nos**).

It's best that you not send it to us.

Da tú (**lo/se**).

Give it to him.

Ya no tiene barba. Afeitó el sábado (**se/la**).

He no longer has a beard. He shaved it off on Saturday.

 Ya **le** expliqué a **ella** lo que tiene que hacer.

No **me** he comprado nada.

Creo que voy a avisar**las** ahora mismo/Creo que **las** voy a avisar ahora mismo.

Es mejor que no **nos** la mandes.

Dá**selo** tú.

Ya no tiene barba. **Se la** afeitó el sábado.

Object pronouns in Spanish go before the verbal sequence. When used with an infinitive or present participle, they can also be attached to it (*avisarlas*); when used with an affirmative command, they must always be attached to it (*Dáselo tú*). Indirect object pronouns must precede direct object pronouns (*nos la mandes, Dáselo, Se la afeitó*).

Quiz: Personal Pronouns

1. Si pudiera hallar una secretaria que supiera hablar español, querría _____ el puesto.

   (A) darle   (C) darla

   (B) le dar   (D) dar le

2. Ana María quiere que Juan sepa la verdad, pero se niega a _____.

   (A) decírlela   (C) decírselos

   (B) decírsela   (D) decírlase

3. He perdido mis maletas y en _____ lo tenía todo.

   (A) la   (C) ella

   (B) las   (D) ellas

4. Será preciso que vayas al concierto con nosotros porque, entre _____ no nos divertiremos sin ti.

   (A) nos   (C) tú y yo

   (B) te y me   (D) ti y mí

5. Cuando tropezaron _____, acababa de salir del cine.

   (A) con mí   (C) conmigo

   (B) con migo   (D) conmi

6. Sus ideas parecen fáciles. Sí, _____ son.

   (A) las   (C) ellas

   (B) lo   (D) la

7.   No _____ pasado mañana.

    (A)   lo hagas   (C)   lo hayan hecho

    (B)   háganlo   (D)   hazlo

8.   Necesito más dinero para asistir al concierto; voy a _____ a mis padres.

    (A)   preguntárselo   (C)   pedírselo

    (B)   preguntarlo   (D)   pedirles

9.   Al ver _____ en la fotografía Elena pensó que había engordado demasiado.

    (A)   nos   (C)   los

    (B)   se   (D)   les

10. Se me _____ todos los apuntes que tomé.

    (A)   olvidé   (C)   olvidaron

    (B)   ha olvidado   (D)   olvidó

ANSWER KEY

1.	(A)	6.	(B)
2.	(B)	7.	(A)
3.	(D)	8.	(C)
4.	(C)	9.	(B)
5.	(C)	10.	(C)

CHAPTER 17

Other Pronouns

17.1 Relative Pronouns

Masculine Singular	Masculine Plural	Feminine Singular	Feminine Plural
que	que	que	que
cual	cuales	cual	cuales
quien	quienes	quien	quienes
cuyo	cuyos	cuya	cuyas

17.1.1 Uses of the Relative Pronouns

a) *Que* (that, which, who, whom) can refer to persons or things.

*El hombre **que** compró la casa...* The man **who** bought the house ...

*El cuadro **que** se vendió...* The picture **that** was sold ...

b) *Que* may follow a few prepositions (*a, de, en, con*) but must be preceded by the definite article when it follows other prepositions (see 18.1 for a list of the simple prepositions in Spanish). Furthermore, when *que* follows a preposition directly, it may only refer to things.

*El libro de **que** te hablé...* The book about **which** I talked to you ...*

El amigo del que te hablé... The friend about **whom** I talked to you ...*

El bolígrafo con que escribo... The (ballpoint) pen with **which** I write ...*

La mujer con la que salía... The woman with **whom** I was going out ...*

* Often in English the use of the relative pronoun is optional. Saying "The book I talked to you about" is equivalent to "The book about which I talked to you." But in Spanish, the use of the relative pronoun is **required**.

c) *Cual* (which, who, whom) also may refer to persons or things, but it is preceded by the definite article. It always agrees in number with its antecedent. (Compare with *cuyo*.)

Vuestra hermana, la cual acababa de llegar... Your sister, **who** had just arrived ...

Las sábanas, las cuales estaban manchadas... The sheets, **which** were stained ...

d) *El cual* (or *el que*) is used instead of *que* or *quien* for greater precision, the article clarifying the antecedent in ambiguous constructions.

Me dio órdenes y consejos, los cuales seguí. He gave me orders and advice, **which** I followed.

In this example in English you cannot distinguish between the feminine *orden* and the masculine *consejo*. The use of *los cuales* in Spanish makes it clear that what the speaker followed was the advice and not necessarily the orders.

e) *El cual* (or *el que*) is used instead of *que* or *quien* after a clause whose sense is parenthetical and simply gives information.

Mi familia tenía varios castillos, los cuales (los que) ya se derrumbaron. My family owned several castles, **which** have already crumbled.

Note: The difference between *el cual* and *el que* is one of formality, *el cual* being more formal and less idiomatic than *el que*.

f)   *El cual* (or *el que*) can always be used after a preposition and is usually used instead of *que* or *quien* when *que* or *quien* would follow a preposition.

*La mujer a **quien** amaba... La mujer a **la que** amaba... La mujer a **la cual** amaba...* The woman (**whom**) he loved...*

*Los temas sobre **los que** discurría... Los temas sobre **los cuales** discurría...* The themes on **which** he discoursed...

*   The preposition *a* in these examples is explained by the use of a personal direct object (it is the personal *a*).

g)   *Cual* (and *que*) may also be preceded by the neuter article *lo,* in which case the antecedent of the pronoun is taken to be the entire preceding idea or clause.

*El criminal fue capturado, **lo cual** (**lo que**) me puso de buen humor.* The criminal was captured, **which** put me in a good mood.

Note: *Lo cual* and *lo que* are not interchangeable when the meaning of the expression is "that which." In this case only *lo que* is grammatically correct.

***Lo que** me molesta es que no pidan disculpas.* **What** (that which) bothers me is that they won't apologize.

h)   *Quien* (who, whom) refers only to persons and always agrees in number with its antecedent.

*Agradecí a mis padres, sin **quienes** nunca habría salido adelante.* I thanked my parents, without **whom** I could never have made it.

i)   *Cuyo* (whose) agrees **not** with its antecedent but with the noun following it. It thus behaves as an adjective.

*Las hormigas **cuyos** escondites destruimos...* The ants **whose** hiding places we destroyed...

*El hombre **cuya** fe nunca vaciló...* The man **whose** faith never faltered...

17.2 Possessive Pronouns

These are closely related to possessive adjectives.

Singular		Plural	
Masculine	Feminine	Masculine	Feminine
el mío	*la mía*	*los míos*	*las mías*
el tuyo	*la tuya*	*los tuyos*	*las tuyas*
el suyo	*la suya*	*los suyos*	*las suyas*
el nuestro	*la nuestra*	*los nuestros*	*las nuestras*
el vuestro	*la vuestra*	*los vuestros*	*las vuestras*
el suyo	*la suya*	*los suyos*	*las suyas*

17.2.1 Uses of the Possessive Pronouns

Possessive pronouns agree in gender and number with the nouns they represent.

Sé que te gustó mi respuesta. I know you liked my answer.
*Sé que te gustó **la mía**.* I know you liked **mine**.
No me contaron sus secretos. They didn't tell me their secrets.
*No me contaron **los suyos**.* They didn't tell me **theirs**.

Note: In the third person singular and plural some ambiguity is likely, since *el suyo* or *los suyos* may refer to different persons. To prevent ambiguity, the possessive pronoun may be replaced by a prepositional complement (*de él, de ellos*, etc.).

*El regalo es **suyo**. El regalo es (**de él, de ella, de Ud., de ellos, de ellas, de Uds.**).* The gift is (**his, hers, yours, theirs**).

17.3 Demonstrative Pronouns

These are closely related to demonstrative adjectives.

Singular		Plural		English
Masculine	Feminine	Masculine	Feminine	
éste	*ésta*	*éstos*	*éstas*	this one these (ones)
ése	*ésa*	*ésos*	*ésas*	that one those (ones)
aquél	*aquélla*	*aquéllos*	*aquéllas*	that one those (ones)

Neuter	
esto	this
eso	that
aquello	that

17.3.1 Uses of the Demonstrative Pronouns

a) They agree in gender and number with the nouns they represent.

Pienso llevarme estos cocos y esas manzanas. I'm thinking of taking these coconuts and those apples.

*Pienso llevarme **éstos** y **aquéllas**.* I'm thinking of taking **these** and **those**.

b) The difference between *ése* and *aquél* is that the former is associated with something close to the person spoken to, whereas the latter is associated with an object remote from both speaker and interlocutor.

*Ése me gusta pero **aquél** me gusta más.* I like **that one** but I like **the one over there** better.

c)   The neuter forms of the possessive pronouns refer to vague and
     general ideas.

Eso le pasó por descuido. **That** is what he got for being careless.

Aquello no tiene solución. **That** has no solution.

Esto es imposible. **This** is impossible.

17.4   Interrogative Pronouns

Interrogative pronouns are the same as relative pronouns, except
that interrogative pronouns have accent marks:

¿qué? what?
¿cuál/es? which?
¿quién/es? who?
¿cuánto/a/os/as? how much? how many?

17.4.1   Uses of the Interrogative Pronouns

These pronouns may be used in both direct and indirect questions.

*¿**Qué** ocurrió ayer?* **What** happened yesterday?

*No sé **qué** ocurrió ayer.* I don't know **what** happened yesterday.

*¿**Cuáles** te gustan más?* **Which** (ones) do you like better?

*No sé **cuáles** me gustan más.* I don't know **which** (ones) I like better.

*Aló, ¿**quién** es?* Hello, **who** is it?

*¿**Cuántas** te has bebido?* **How many** (drinks) have you had?

Problem Solving Examples:

Q Fill in the blanks using the correct possessive or interrogative pronouns:

Este paquete es el _____ (**mine**); aquél otro es el _____ (**hers**).

¿_____ (**Which ones**) te gustan más? ¿Las grandes o las pequeñas?

No sé _____ (**who**) es el responsable ni _____ (**how many**) veces había ocurrido antes.

A mío, suyo, Cuáles, quién, cuántas.

This package is mine; that other one is hers.

Which ones do you like most? The big ones or the small ones?

I don't know who is the responsible one or how many times it had happened before.

Both *mío* and *suyo* must agree with *paquete*. In the second sentence, the plural *cuáles* is required by the context. *Cuántas* agrees with the feminine *veces*. All three interrogatives must have written accents.

Q Choose the appropriate relative or demonstrative pronouns from those provided:

La persona a (**cual/la que**) se lo pregunté no lo sabía.

El vecino con (**que/quien**) me viste es muy simpático.

Tu hermana, a (**cual/la cual**) aún no conozco, llamó el otro día.

Haz (**lo que/lo cual**) quieras.

Es la mejor oportunidad (**que/quien**) has tenido.

(**Esto/Ésta**) es lo mejor que pudo pasar.

Estas sillas no me gustan; prefiero (**ésos/aquéllas**).

A la que, quien, la cual, lo que, que, Esto, aquéllas.

The person whom I asked didn't know it.

The neighbor who you saw me with is very nice.

Your sister, who I still don't know, called the other day.

Do what you want.

It's the best opportunity that you've had.

That is the best thing that could happen.

I don't like these chairs; I prefer those.

Both *que* and *cual* need to be preceded by an article when they are used after a preposition (*a la que se lo pregunté, a la cual aún no conozco*). In the second sentence, *quien* will therefore be the only possible choice after the preposition *con*. In *Haz lo que quieras*, the option *cual* is not possible since *cual* can never be used unless the antecedent is explicitly present in the sentence. *Quien* can only refer to people and never to things such as *oportunidad*. In the next to last example, the pronoun *esto* agrees with *lo mejor* since they both refer to the same thing. In the last sentence, *aquéllas* refers to *sillas* and must therefore agree with it.

Quiz: Other Pronouns

1. La puerta por _____ entraste es del siglo XI.

   (A) qué

   (B) lo que

   (C) que

   (D) la cual

2. Los señores de _____ te hablo son extranjeros aquí.

   (A) que

   (B) cuales

   (C) cuyos

   (D) quienes

3. Marta, _____ hijo es ingeniero, vive en Buenos Aires.

    (A) quien   (C) de quien

    (B) cuya   (D) cuyo

4. _____ que no puedo entender es por qué se fue sin decir adiós.

    (A) Lo   (C) El

    (B) Ello   (D) Esto

5. Yo tengo mi tarea y Juan tiene _____.

    (A) mía   (C) la suya

    (B) el suyo   (D) el de él

6. Muéstreme otro apartamento, no me gusta _____.

    (A) esto   (C) esté

    (B) este   (D) éste

7. ¿Qué es _____?

    (A) éste   (C) ésto

    (B) esto   (D) ésta

8. ¿_____ son los meses del año?

    (A) Cuál   (C) Qué

    (B) Cuáles   (D) De quién

9. Mi hermana es más alta que _____.

    (A) la suya   (C) su

    (B) el suyo   (D) mía

10. El padre de Martín siempre le había dicho: _____ tienen una educación, tienen el poder.

    (A) los que   (C) cuales

    (B) que   (D) los quienes

ANSWER KEY

1.	(D)	6.	(D)
2.	(D)	7.	(B)
3.	(D)	8.	(B)
4.	(A)	9.	(A)
5.	(C)	10.	(A)

Prepositions and Conjunctions

18.1 Prepositions

Prepositions are words or phrases that relate words to one another, especially nouns to verbs, to adjectives, and to other nouns.

Here is a basic list of prepositions:

a—to	*excepto*—except
bajo—under	*hacia*—toward
con—with	*hasta*—until, as far as, to
contra—against	*para*—for
de—of	*por*—for
desde—from, since	*según*—according to
durante—during	*sin*—without
en—in, at, on	*sobre*—on, upon, over, above
entre—between, among	

*Conozco la América **desde** el desierto de California **hasta** la Patagonia.* I know the Americas* **from** the California desert **to** Patagonia.

*	In Spanish, *la América* can pertain to North and South America. When describing the United States, *los Estados Unidos* is used.

Desde siempre existe la envidia entre hermanos. Envy **between** brothers has always existed (has existed **since** forever).

Lléname el vaso hasta aquí. Fill my glass **up to** here.

Dejé el sobre sobre la mesa. I left the envelope **on** the table.

Compound prepositions are also common in Spanish. They are formed by adding *de* to certain adverbs:

además de—besides	*dentro de*—within
alrededor de—around	*después de*—after (time)
antes de—before	*detrás de*—behind
a pesar de— in spite of	*encima de*—on top of
cerca de—near	*enfrente de*—across, opposite
debajo de—under	*fuera de*—outside of
delante de—in front of	*lejos de*—far from

18.1.1 *Para* vs. *Por*

In general, *por* expresses the ideas contained in "for the sake of," "through," and "exchange"; whereas *para* expresses destination, purpose, end, and intention.

a) *Por* means "through"; *para* refers to destination:

Iba por el parque. I was walking **through** the park.

Iba para el parque. I was **on my way to** the park.

b) *Por* refers to motive; *para* refers to purpose or end:

Lo hizo por mí. He did it **for** me (for my sake, on my behalf).

El artesano hizo una vasija para mí. The artisan made a vase **for** me.

c) *Por* expresses the idea of exchange:

Lo cambié por una camisa. I exchanged it **for** a shirt.

d) *Por* denotes a span of time; *para* designates an endpoint in time:

Los exiliados caminaron por tres días y tres noches. The exiles walked **for** (during, for the span of) three days and three nights.

*El traje estará listo **para** el lunes.* The suit will be ready **by** Monday.

e)   *Para* translates to "in order to":

*Fui a su casa **para** hablar con él.* I went to his house **in order to** speak to him.

f)   *Por* and *para* have set meanings in certain idiomatic constructions:

***por** ejemplo*—for example

***por** lo menos*—at least

***para** siempre*—forever

*No es **para** tanto.* It's not that serious.

18.1.2 Prepositions with Verbs

Many verbs are associated with or supplemented by certain prepositions whose meanings may differ from English usage. A list of the most common ones follows:

acabar de—to have just (done something)
acercarse a—to approach
acostumbrarse a—to get used to
alegrarse de—to be glad to
aprender a—to learn to
ayudar a—to help to
casarse con—to marry
comenzar a—to start to
consistir en—to consist of
contar con—to count on
dejar de—to stop
despedirse de—to say goodbye to
disfrutar de—to enjoy
enamorarse de—to fall in love with
esforzarse por—to strive to
estar para—to be about to

estar por—to be in favor of
fijarse en—to notice
oler a—to smell of
pensar en—to think of
ponerse a—to set oneself to
quedar en—to agree to
reírse de—to laugh at
reparar en—to notice
saber a—to taste like (of)
salir a—to take after
servir de—to serve as
soñar con—to dream of
tratar de—to try to
vestirse de—to dress like

*Anoche **soñé con** ella.* Last night I **dreamed of** her.

*La fe me **ayudó a** sobrevivir.* Faith **helped** me (**to**) survive.

*Me quiero **casar con** ella.* I want **to marry** her. (I want **to get married to** her.)

*Ya no **pienso en** ti.* I don't **think of** you anymore.

***Trataré de** ser mejor amigo.* I'll **try to** be a better friend.

***Dejé de** ir a la escuela.* I **stopped** going to school.

18.2 Conjunctions

Conjunctions are words or phrases that connect clauses to one another. The following is a basic list of conjunctions:

o (u)—or
y (e)—and
pero, mas, sino que—but
ni—nor, neither
que—that
si—if, whether

18.2.1 Uses of the Basic Conjunctions

a)   *O* changes to *u* in front of words beginning with *o* or *ho*:

*No sé si lo dijo Roberto **u** Horacio.* I don't know whether Roberto **or** Horacio said it.

b)   *Y* changes to *e* in front of words beginning with *i* or *hi*:

*Padre **e** hijo viajaban juntos.* Father **and** son were traveling together.

Note: *Y* does not change in front of *y* or *hie*:

*fuego **y** hielo*—fire **and** ice

*tú **y** yo*—you **and** I

c)   *Ni* is the counterpart of *y*. It is often repeated in a sentence to mean "neither...nor":

ni Juan ni Marta—**neither** Juan **nor** Marta

18.2.2 *Pero* vs. *Sino*

Pero, mas, and *sino* mean "but." (*Más* with an accent mark, however, is an adverb meaning "more.") *Pero* and *mas* are interchangeable, but *pero* and *sino* have different uses. *Sino* (or *sino que*) has the sense of "rather" or "on the contrary."

*No dije "roca" **sino** "foca."* I didn't say "rock" **but** "seal."

*No vino para quedarse **sino que** vino y se fue.** She didn't come to stay **but** came and left.

*Mi abuelo ya murió **pero** me dejó un buen recuerdo.* My grandfather already died **but** he left me good memories.

*   When the contrast is between clauses with different verb forms, *que* is introduced.

18.2.3 Correlative Conjunctions

Conjunctions such as *ni... ni* are not uncommon in Spanish. Other pairs are:

o... o—either...or
ya... ya—whether...or, sometimes...sometimes

*Decídete. **O** te vas **o** haces lo que te digo.* Make up your mind.
   Either you leave **or** you do as I say.

18.2.4 Conjunctive Phrases

a fin de que—in order that
a medida que—as, according to
a menos que—unless
así que—so that, as soon as
aunque—even though, although
conque—so, therefore
con tal (de) que—as long as, provided that
de modo (manera) que—so that
desde que—since
en caso (de) que—in case that
hasta que—until
luego que—as soon as
mientras (que)—while
para que—in order that
porque—because
puesto que—since
siempre que—whenever
ya que—since

*A **medida que** pasaban las horas Laura se desesperaba.* **As** the
   hours passed, Laura grew more desperate.

*La he conocido **desde que** era niña.* I have known her **since** she
   was a child.

Ya que no tienes hambre, no vayas al restaurante. **Since** you're not hungry, don't go to the restaurant.

Problem Solving Examples:

Complete with the appropriate prepositions and conjunctions:

Rosario _____ Iván van a estar _____ viaje _____ lunes _____ domingo. No quieren viajar en coche _____ en tren. Han quedado _____ ir en bicicleta para poder disfrutar _____ paisaje. Yo he tratado _____ hacerles cambiar de idea _____ no lo he conseguido, _____ que les he dicho que no contaran _____ nosotros a _____ que fuesen en coche.

e, de, de, a, ni, en, del, de, pero, así, con, menos.

Rosario and Ivan are going to be on vacation from Monday to Sunday. They don't want to travel by car or by train. They have settled on going by bicycle in order to be able to enjoy the countryside. I've tried to make them change their minds but I haven't been able to, so that I've told them not to count on us unless they go by car.

When the next word starts with an *i-/hi-*, the conjunction *y* is substituted by *e*. The names of the days of the week can be used without articles in the expression *de... a* but not in *desde... hasta. No/ni... ni* means "neither...nor." *Estar de viaje, quedar en, disfrutar de, tratar de,* and *contar con* are all verbs which need to be accompanied by specific prepositions in order to convey certain meanings. *Así que* means "so that" and *a menos que* means "unless."

Choose the correct prepositions and conjunctions:

Desde enero, Pedro trabaja (**para/por**) la compañía de sus tíos y va a seguir haciéndolo (**para/por**) unos meses. Necesita ahorrar dinero (**para/por**) comprarse un coche nuevo. Quiere que el coche le dure (**para/por**) lo menos unos diez años. El cree que tendrá el dinero (**para/por**) noviembre.

Pedro no quiere pagar demasiado (**para/por**) el coche. No quiere un coche grande (**pero/sino que**) quiere comprar el más pequeño que encuentre.

    para, por, para, por, para, por, sino que.

Since January, Pedro's been working for his uncle's company and is going to continue doing it for some months. He needs to save money to buy himself a new car. He wants the car to last him for at least 10 years. He believes he'll have the money by November. Pedro doesn't want to pay too much for the car. He doesn't want a big car but wants to buy the smallest one that he finds.

Trabaja para indicates destination or purpose of the action. *Por unos meses* indicates a period of time whereas *para noviembre* indicates a deadline. *Ahorrar dinero para* means "to save money in order to" and indicates the intention of the action. *Por lo menos* is an idiomatic construction. *Por el coche* refers to an idea of exchange. The Spanish translation of "rather, on the contrary" is *sino que.*

Quiz: Prepositions and Conjunctions

1.   La silla estaba _____ la mesa.

    (A) antes de   (C) en cuanto a

    (B) detrás de   (D) después de

2.   Mi viejo amigo Fernando trabaja _____ la Compañía Equis.

    (A) por   (C) cerca

    (B) a   (D) para

3.   Como era natural, el perro salió _____ la puerta.

    (A) para   (C) a

    (B) por   (D) de

4.   De niño siempre soñaba _____ ser rico.

    (A) de   (C) con

    (B) para   (D) en

5.   _____ escribir el ensayo.

    (A) Empezaron   (C) Comenzaron

    (B) Se pusieron a   (D) Se olvidaron

6.   No va a comprar el coche _____ venderlo.

    (A) pero   (C) sino que

    (B) pero que   (D) sino

7.   ¿Cuánto dinero me dará Ud. _____ mi trabajo?

    (A) por   (C) de

    (B) en   (D) para

8.   Tienes que llamar a tu casa _____ que no se preocupen.

    (A) para   (C) hacia

    (B) por   (D) desde

9.   Es un buen libro _____ aprender a cocinar.

    (A) por   (C) para

    (B) con   (D) en

10. Hace cinco siglos, cuando Fernando _____ Isabel reinaban en España, Colón descubrió un mundo desconocido más tarde nombrado América.

    (A) y   (C) u

    (B) e   (D) de

ANSWER KEY

1.	(B)		6.	(D)
2.	(D)		7.	(A)
3.	(B)		8.	(A)
4.	(C)		9.	(C)
5.	(B)		10.	(B)

CHAPTER 19

Affirmatives and Negatives

19.1 Forms of the Affirmatives

sí—yes
algo—something
alguien—someone, somebody

alguno*—some, any
siempre—always
cualquier (a)—any, anyone

* When *alguno* follows a noun, it is a **negative** interchangeable with *ninguno*:

*No he visto periódico **alguno** desde que llegué.* I have **not** seen **any** newspaper since I arrived.

*No he visto **ningún** periódico desde que llegué.* I have **not** seen **any** newspaper since I arrived. (I have seen **no** newspaper since I arrived.)

19.2 Uses of the Affirmatives

a) *Sí* (yes) must be distinguished from *si* (if) at all times:

*¿Tienes dinero? **Sí, si** te hace falta.* Do you have money? **Yes, if** you need it.

Sí may also function as the affirmative **"did"** in English:

*Yo **sí** vine cuando me llamaste.* I **did** come when you called me.

Sí may also emphasize a question, in which case it means "right?" in English:

Te gustó la sopa, ¿sí? You liked the soup, **right**?

b) Except for the exception noted in 19.1, *alguno, algo, alguien,* and *siempre* function as they do in English. *Alguno,* however, may adopt different forms:

*¿Tienes **alguna** razón para odiarme?* Do you have **any** reason to hate me?

***Algunos** llegaron a tiempo pero otros se retrasaron.* **Some** arrived on time but others were late.

*¿Hay **algún** inconveniente para llevar a cabo ese plan?* Is there **any** problem in carrying out that plan?

In the last example *alguno* loses the final "o"—and gains an accent mark—because it stands in front of a masculine singular noun. This is also true of *ninguno.*

c) *Cualquier(a)* means "any" in the context of a choice:

*¿Cuál de ésos quiere? **Cualquiera**.* Which of those do you want? **Whichever**.

Cualquier hombre o mujer tendría miedo.* **Any** man or woman would be afraid.

* *Cualquiera* drops the last letter (*-a*) before any singular noun.

19.3 Forms of the Negatives

no—no	*nunca*—never
nada—nothing	*jamás*—never
nadie—nobody, no one	*tampoco*—either, neither
ninguno—none, neither	*ni*—not even, nor

19.4 Uses of the Negatives

a) A negative may either precede or follow the verb. **If it precedes the verb, *no* is not required, but if it follows the verb, *no* must be placed immediately before the verb** (or the reflexive or object pronoun):

Nada vi. I saw **nothing**.
No vi nada. I did **not** see **anything**.

Con nadie hablé. I spoke to **no one**.
No hablé con nadie. I did **not** speak with **anyone**.

Nunca me lo imaginé. I **never** imagined it.
No me lo imaginé nunca. I **never** imagined it.

Jamás le ofrecí dinero. I **never** offered him money.
No le ofrecí dinero jamás. I **never** offered him money.

Tampoco vino Pedro. Pedro did not come **either**.
No vino Pedro tampoco. Pedro did not come **either**.

This means that in Spanish the double negative is grammatical whereas in English it is not. The double negative may also become a multiple negative:

No dije nunca nada a nadie. I **never** said **anything** to **anyone**.

b) *Ninguno* can be masculine or feminine but is no longer used in the plural:

Ninguno de ellos compareció. **None** of them showed up.

No queda ningún hombre de fe sobre la tierra. There is **no** man of faith left on the earth. (There are no men of faith left on Earth. There aren't any men of faith left on Earth.)

In this example *ninguno* loses the final "*o*" because it precedes a masculine singular noun.

Ninguna mujer te va a olvidar. **No** woman will forget you.

Affirmatives and Negatives

Sometimes *ninguno* is replaced by **ni uno** in order to emphasize the negation:

*No tengo **ni un** centavo.* I don't have a cent (to my name).

c)   The difference between *nunca* and *jamás* is one of emphasis.

Nunca *quiero volver a verte.* I **never** want to see you again.

Jamás *quiero volver a verte.* I don't want to see you **ever** again.

d)   *Ni* may be used by itself, it can be a correlative conjunction (*ni... ni*), or it can be correlated with *tampoco* or *siquiera*. But it can also function like *no* and precede a verb followed by another negative.

*No me convenció su argumento **ni** me convencerá el tuyo.* His argument didn't convince me, **nor** will yours.

***Ni** tu amigo va a reconocer tu disfraz.* **Not even** your friend will recognize your disguise.

***Ni** el policía **ni** el asaltador resultaron heridos.* **Neither** the policeman **nor** the assailant was hurt.

*Esa respuesta no es correcta **ni tampoco** esa otra.* That answer is not right and **neither** is that other one.

***Ni siquiera** te molestaste en saludarme.* You did **not even** bother to greet me.

***Ni** vino **nadie** a buscarte.* **Nor** did **anyone** come looking for you.

Problem Solving Examples:

Choose the correct forms:

No he visto a (**alguien/nadie**) desde que llegué. Parece que casi (**alguno/ningún**) invitado ha llegado todavía. Ahí llega (**alguna/alguien**) muchacha. (**Siempre/Nunca**) había asistido tan poca gente a esta celebración. No ha venido Marisa (**no/ni**) (**tampoco/también**) ha venido su hermano.

nadie, ningún, alguna, Nunca, ni, tampoco.

I haven't seen anyone since I arrived. It seems that almost no guest has arrived yet. Here comes some girl. Never had so few attended this celebration. Marisa hasn't come nor has her brother come either.

In Spanish, double and also multiple negatives are used in the same sentence; therefore, all negative words in a negative statement must be used in their negative forms (*no he visto a nadie..., no ha venido Marisa ni tampoco...*). However, when a negative expression precedes the verb, the word *no* must be omitted (*ningún invitado ha llegado..., Nunca había asistido...*). The abbreviated forms *algún* and *ningún* must be used in front of masculine singular nouns (*ningún invitado*). *Alguien* and *nadie* can only be used alone and never with other nouns (*Ahí llega alguna muchacha*). *No/ni... ni* means "neither... nor."

 Change the following sentences into their negative/affirmative equivalents. All the words in bold lettering must be changed and other words may need to be added:

¿Quieres beber **algo**?

Do you want to drink something?

No te puedo hacer **ninguna** promesa.

I can't make you any promises.

Jamás voy al teatro los domingos.

I never go to the theater on Sundays.

Tiene **algunos** sobrinos **y también** tiene **un** nieto.

He has some nieces and nephews and also has one grandson.

 ¿**No** quieres beber **nada**?

Don't you want to drink anything?

Te puedo hacer **alguna** promesa.

I can make you a promise.

Siempre voy al teatro los domingos.

I always go to the theater on Sundays.

No tiene **ningún** sobrino **ni tampoco** tiene **ningún** nieto.

He doesn't have a niece or nephew nor a grandson either.

The word *no* must precede the verb in both the first and last sentences in the exercise. The words *algunos sobrinos* in the last sentence must be replaced by the singular *ningún sobrino* since there is not a plural negative form. The negative equivalent to *un* can only be *ningún* (or *ni un*).

CHAPTER 20

Numerals

20.1 Cardinal and Ordinal Forms of Numerals

The cardinal and ordinal forms of numbers in Spanish are as follows:

Cardinal Numbers

1	*uno/a*	16	*diez y seis*
2	*dos*	17	*diez y siete*
3	*tres*	18	*diez y ocho*
4	*cuatro*	19	*diez y nueve*
5	*cinco*	20	*veinte*
6	*seis*	30	*treinta*
7	*siete*	40	*cuarenta*
8	*ocho*	50	*cincuenta*
9	*nueve*	100	*cien(to/a)*
10	*diez*	101	*ciento uno*
11	*once*	200	*doscientos/as*
12	*doce*	500	*quinientos/as*
13	*trece*	700	*setecientos/as*
14	*catorce*	900	*novecientos/as*
15	*quince*	1000	*mil*
		1,000,000	*un millón*

Note: The cardinal numbers from 16 to 29 may be written together: *dieciséis, diecisiete, dieciocho, diecinueve, veintiuno, veintinueve.*

Beyond 30, cardinal numbers are written: *treinta y uno, treinta y dos,* etc.

Ordinal Numbers

1	*primero*	6	*sexto*
2	*segundo*	7	*séptimo*
3	*tercero*	8	*octavo*
4	*cuarto*	9	*noveno (nono)*
5	*quinto*	10	*décimo*

20.2 Cardinal Numbers

a) Only *uno* and the compounds of *cien(to)* (such as 200, 210, 500, 300,001, etc.) are variable. All other cardinal numbers are invariable. *Uno* drops the final "*o*" in front of masculine nouns; *cien* is preferred over *ciento* except in front of another numeral **that is not *mil* or *millón*:**

Un hombre, sólo uno, sabe el secreto. **One** man, only **one**, knows the secret.

Una mujer casada y unas monjas están hablando. **A** married woman and **some** nuns are talking.

Note that the cardinal number *uno* is the same as the indefinite article.

Cien mil soldados lucharon en la batalla; sólo ciento veinte murieron. **One hundred** thousand soldiers fought in the battle; only **one hundred** and twenty died.

Enviamos quinientas invitaciones. We sent out **five hundred** invitations.

b) *Cien* and *mil* do not take (as in English) the indefinite article but *millón* does. *Millón* is also followed by the preposition *de*:

Me gané un millón de dólares pero tengo mil deudas. I won **a million** dollars, but I have **a thousand** debts.

20.3 Ordinal Numbers

a) Ordinal numbers are variable in gender and number:

*Eres la **cuarta** persona que me pregunta lo mismo.* You are the **fourth** person to ask me the same thing.

*Los **primeros** en irse fueron los últimos en llegar.* The **first** to leave were the last to arrive.

b) *Primero* and *tercero* drop their final "*o*" in front of masculine singular nouns:

*el **tercer** ojo*—the **third** eye   *el **primer** chico*—the **first** boy

c) Ordinal numbers precede nouns except when referring to kings, dukes, popes, or other kinds of succession:

*Juan Carlos **Primero** es el rey de España.* Juan Carlos **I** is the king of Spain.

*Juan Pablo **Segundo** es el papa.* John Paul **II** is the pope.

d) Usage dictates that after *décimo* no more ordinal numbers are used; they are replaced by cardinal numbers situated after the nouns:

*La **décima** carrera fue más emocionante que la (carrera) **once**.* The **tenth** race was more exciting than the **eleventh** (race).

*España no tuvo un rey llamado Pedro **Quince**.* Spain did not have a king named Pedro **the Fifteenth**.

Note: The definite article (the) is omitted before the number.

20.4 Dates

Contrary to English usage, **cardinal** numbers are used to indicate dates **except in the case of the first of the month**:

*el **primero** de mayo*—the first of May
*el **dos** de mayo*—the second of May

*el **tres** de mayo*—the third of May
*el **diez** de mayo*—the tenth of May
*el **treinta** de mayo*—the thirtieth of May

The year may be added to these dates by inserting the preposition *de*:

*el tres de octubre **de** 1951*—October 3, 1951
*el veinte de abril **de** este año*—April 20th of this year

In dating letters the definite article is omitted.

It's common to replace *de este año* by *del corriente* (of the current year):

el veintiocho de febrero del corriente—February 28th of this year

"What day is today?" may be rendered literally as *¿Qué día es hoy?* or idiomatically as *¿A cómo estamos (hoy)?* The latter expression implies a date as an answer, not just the day of the week:

¿A cómo estamos? Estamos a trece de junio. What's the date? It is June 13th.

¿Qué día es hoy? Hoy es lunes. What day is today? Today is Monday.

20.5 Arithmetical Signs

+ *más*
− *menos*
× *por*
÷ *dividido por*

2 + 2 is *dos **más** dos;* 10 ÷ 5 is *diez **dividido por** cinco;* 3 × 3 is *tres **por** tres.*

20.6 Collective Numerals

un par—a pair
una decena—ten

una docena—a dozen
una quincena—fifteen, two weeks*
una veintena—twenty
una centena (un centenar)—hundred
un millar—thousand

* Unlike in English, two weeks in Spanish is equivalent to 15 days, not 14, because Sunday is counted 3 times.

*Pagan cada **quincena**.* They pay every **two weeks**.

*El libro tiene una **centena** de poemas.* The book has **one hundred** poems.

*Un **millar** de personas.* A **thousand** people.

Note: *Quincenal* is an adjective made from *quincena*. Other similar numerical adjectives are *semanal* (weekly), *mensual* (monthly), *semestral* (half-yearly), and *anual* (yearly).

*Una publicación **quincenal**.* A **biweekly** publication.

*Una revista **semestra**.* A **half-yearly** magazine.

20.7 Fractions

1/2	*un medio*	1/3	*un tercio*
1/4	*un cuarto*	1/5	*un quinto*
1/6	*un sexto*	1/7	*un séptimo*
1/8	*un octavo*	1/9	*un noveno*
1/10	*un décimo*		

Two-thirds is either *dos tercios* or *las dos terceras partes;* three-fourths is either *tres cuartos* or *las tres cuartas partes.*

Un medio is only used in arithmetical calculations; the adjective meaning "half" is *medio/a;* the noun meaning "half" is *la mitad*:

*Trabajamos sólo **medio** día hoy.* Today we only worked **half** a day.

***La mitad** del electorado no votó.* **Half** of the electorate did not vote.

Problem Solving Examples:

 Translate the numerals into the correct Spanish equivalent for each context:

_____ (**245**) personas asistieron al encuentro.

Había _____ (**100,001**) invitados.

Tiene _____ (**160**) palomas.

El premio será _____ (**1,000,000**) de liras.

Él fue mi _____ (**first**) novio y tú eres el _____ (**third**).

Compra _____ (**a dozen**) de huevos y _____ (**half**) kilogramo de patatas.

 Doscientas cuarenta y cinco, cien mil un, ciento sesenta, un millón, primer, tercero, una docena, medio.

Two hundred and forty-five persons attended the meeting.

There were 100,001 guests.

He has 160 pigeons.

The prize will be one million lira.

He was my first boyfriend and you're the third.

He buys a dozen eggs and half a kilo of potatoes.

Doscientos/-as must agree with the noun that follows. *Cien* and not *ciento* must be used in front of *mil* and *millón*. However, *ciento* is used in front of all other numerals (*ciento sesenta palomas*). The abbreviated forms *un* and *primer* must be used in front of all masculine nouns such as *invitados* and *novio*. When "half" is used as an adjective, its Spanish translation is *medio*.

Choose the correct numerals:

Sólo quiero (**el medio/la mitad**) de ese bocadillo.

Me basta con un (**tercero/tercio**) de las explicaciones que me has dado.

Es la (**quinta/quinto**) revista (**quincena/quincenal**) que publican aquí.

Hoy es el (**cuarto/cuatro**) de abril.

la mitad, tercio, quinta, quincenal, cuatro.

I only want half of that sandwich.

I'm okay with a third of the explanations you've given me.

It's the fifth biweekly magazine that they publish here.

Today is April 4th.

When "half" is used as a substantive, its Spanish translation is *la mitad*. The fraction "a third" is rendered by the Spanish *un tercio*. All ordinals agree with the nouns they modify (*quinta revista*). *Quincenal* ("biweekly") is an adjective that goes with the noun *revista*. Cardinal numbers such as *cuarto* are used in Spanish to indicate the date.

Quiz: Affirmatives and Negatives–Numerals

1. Viene a vernos _____.

    (A) nunca   (C) nadie

    (B) alguien   (D) jamás

2. Cuando salimos del cine, no vimos _____ taxi.

    (A) ningún   (C) nada

    (B) algún   (D) ninguno

3. Sin mirar _____, los reos se presentaron ante el juez.

    (A) a nadie   (C) nadie

    (B) a alguien   (D) alguien

4. ¿Tienes algunos amigos íntimos? No, no tengo _____.

    (A) ningunos   (C) ningún

    (B) nadie   (D) ninguno

5. Nadie va con ellos, ni con Juan _____.

    (A) ni   (C) nadie

    (B) tampoco   (D) también

6. Había _____ millones de personas que compraron billetes.

    (A) cientos   (C) ciento

    (B) cien   (D) cientas

7. Había (231) _____ mujeres en el estadio.

    (A) doscientos treinta y uno

    (B) doscientas treinta y uno

    (C) doscientas treinta y una

    (D) doscientas treinta y unas

8. Fueron los _____ en salir del estadio.

    (A) unos   (C) primer

    (B) primos   (D) primeros

9. Cuando fuimos a vivir en la capital, conseguimos un apartamento hermoso en el _____ piso de un edificio moderno.

    (A) tercero   (C) tercio

    (B) primero   (D) tercer

10. Solamente _____ los asistentes ha estado en la clausura.

    (A) el medio   (C) las mitades

    (B) un medio de   (D) la mitad de

ANSWER KEY

1.	(B)	6.	(B)
2.	(A)	7.	(C)
3.	(A)	8.	(D)
4.	(D)	9.	(D)
5.	(B)	10.	(D)

CHAPTER 21

Basic Vocabulary

21.1 Fundamental Spanish Words

This chapter lists some fundamental Spanish words with their English translations. These words do not include cognates or idioms and are grouped thematically. An effort has been made to exclude words defined somewhere else in this book unless they firmly belong under the rubrics used. The definite articles indicate each word's gender.

La Familia—The Family

el bisabuelo—great-grandfather
la bisabuela—great-grandmother
el abuelo—grandfather
la abuela—grandmother
el padre—father
la madre—mother
el tío—uncle
la tía—aunt
el hermano—brother
la hermana—sister
el hijo—son
la hija—daughter
el nieto—grandson
la nieta—granddaughter
el sobrino—nephew
la sobrina—niece

Los Colores—Colors

el azul—blue
el rosa (rosado)—pink
el rojo (colorado)—red
el marrón (pardo, café)—
  brown

el negro—black
el blanco—white
el amarillo—yellow
el morado (violeta)—purple

La Comida—Food

el arroz—rice
el plátano—plantain, banana
el pan—bread
el agua—water
la mantequilla—butter
el queso—cheese
las aceitunas—olives
el vino—wine
la carne—meat
el tocino—bacon
el jamón—ham
el pescado—fish
el café—coffee
la leche—milk
la cerveza—beer
la ensalada—salad

las verduras (legumbres) —
  vegetables
la lechuga—lettuce
la espinaca—spinach
el choclo (maíz)—corn
las papas (patatas)—
  potatoes
el postre—dessert
la torta—cake
la manzana—apple
la pera—pear
el durazno—peach
las uvas—grapes
la sandía—watermelon
las fresas—strawberries

Las Profesiones—The Professions

el ingeniero—engineer
el médico—physician
el cirujano—surgeon
el enfermero—nurse
el abogado—lawyer
el técnico—technician
el químico—chemist
el físico—physicist

el juez—judge
el periodista—journalist
el policía—policeman
el sastre—tailor
el hombre de negocios—
  businessman
el mecánico—mechanic
el agricultor—farmer

el vendedor—salesman
el dependiente—store clerk
el jefe—boss
el cartero—mailman
el locutor—announcer

el cantante—singer
el cineasta—film director (*auteur*) or producer
el político—politician
el mecanógrafo—typist

Los Animales — Animals

el perro—dog
el gato—cat
el ciervo (venado)—deer
la oveja—sheep
la cabra—goat
la vaca—cow
el cerdo (chancho, puerco, marrano)—pig
el caballo—horse
el toro—bull
el conejo—rabbit

la tortuga—turtle
el ratón—mouse
la ardilla—squirrel
el pájaro—bird
el gallo—rooster
la gallina—hen
el pollo—chicken
el pavo—turkey
el pez (pescado)—fish
el tiburón—shark
la ballena—whale

La Vida Urbana — City Life

la calle—street
el callejón—alley
la bocacalle—intersection
la avenida—avenue
el centro—downtown
la plaza de estacionamiento—parking lot
estacionarse—to park
el ómnibus (autobús, microbús; la guagua, in Cuba; *el camión,* in Mexico)—bus
el subterráneo (el metro)—subway

la plaza—square
la acera (vereda)—sidewalk
el cine—movie theater
el jardín—garden
manejar (conducir, guiar)—to drive
el edificio—building
la puerta—door
la ventana—window
la entrada—entrance, lobby
el ascensor—elevator
las escaleras—stairs
el correo—the mail (system)

Actividades Comunes — Common Activities

nacer—to be born
morir—to die
beber (*tomar*)—to drink
emborracharse—to get drunk
comer—to eat
dormir—to sleep
soñar—to dream
levantarse (*pararse*)—to
get up
sentarse—to sit down
caminar (*andar*)—to walk
detenerse (*pararse*)—to stop
subir—to go up

bajar—to go down
regresar (*volver*)—to return
salir—to go out
viajar—to travel
hablar (*conversar*)—to talk
callar—to be silent
comprar—to buy
vender—to sell
deber—to owe
cansarse—to grow (get)
tired
enfadarse (*enojarse, molestarse*)—to get angry

Los Deportes — Sports

nadar—to swim
la pesca—fishing
el alpinismo—mountain
climbing

el paracaidismo—parachuting
el fútbol—soccer
el árbitro—the referee

La Tecnología — Technology

el ordenador—computer
el disco duro—hard disk
el disco flexible—floppy disk
el teclado—keyboard
la impresora—printer

el, la radio—radio
el televisor—TV set
la televisión—television
el tocadiscos—record player
la grabadora—tape recorder

Las Partes del Cuerpo — Parts of the Body

la cabeza—head
el cabello (*pelo*)—hair
la frente—forehead
la oreja—ear
la nariz—nose

el ojo—eye
la boca—mouth
el diente—tooth
la lengua—tongue
el labio—lip

las pestañas—eyelashes
los párpados—eyelids
el cuello—neck
los hombros—shoulders
la espalda—back
el pecho—chest
los brazos—arms
el codo—elbow
la muñeca—wrist
la mano—hand

los dedos—fingers
las uñas—fingernails
la cintura (el talle)—waist
los muslos—thighs
las caderas—hips
los músculos—muscles
la rodilla—knee
el tobillo—ankle
el talón—heel

Los Objetos Domésticos—Domestic Objects

la lámpara—lamp
el sillón—armchair
el velador—night table
la cama—bed
la sala—living room
la silla—chair
la mesa—table
el comedor—dining room
el dormitorio (la alcoba)—
   bedroom
la cómoda (el tocador)—
   dresser
el patio—yard
el jardín—garden
la cocina—kitchen
*el refrigerador, la heladera
   (nevera)*—refrigerator

los vasos—glasses
las tazas—cups
el horno—oven; furnace
la (el) microondas—micro-
   wave oven
el techo—roof; ceiling
la chimenea—fireplace;
   chimney
el baño—bathroom
el espejo—mirror
el lavatorio—sink
la tina (bañera)—bathtub
la ducha—shower
la toalla—towel
el grifo (la llave)—tap
el conmutador—(light)
   switch

Problem Solving Examples:

 Make the correct choices of vocabulary:

Mi (**sobrina/tía**) es todavía muy pequeña.

Me gusta más el (**tocino/vino**) tinto que el (**blanco/negro**).

Son (**abogados/agricultores**) porque les gustan mucho los (**caballos/tiburones**).

 sobrina, vino, blanco, agricultores, caballos.

My niece is still very small.

I like red wine more than white.

They're farmers because they like horses a lot.

Sobrina means "niece." Wine (*vino*) can either be *blanco, tinto,* or *rosado. Agricultores* means "farmers" and *caballos* means "horses."

 Translate the missing words:

Este _____ (**elevator**) está ya muy viejo. Subamos por las _____ (**stairs**).

Ella siempre _____ (**dreams**) que _____ (**walks**) por un bosque muy frondoso.

A mi primo le gusta tanto _____ (**to swim**) como jugar con el _____ (**computer**).

Me duelen los _____ (**shoulders**) y las _____ (**knees**).

Este dormitorio necesita una _____ (**dresser**) y un _____ (**mirror**).

ascensor, escaleras, sueña, camina/anda, nadar, ordenador, hombros, rodillas, cómoda, espejo.

This elevator is already very old. Let's go up the stairs.

She always dreams she is walking through a leafy forest.

My cousin likes to swim as much as play with the computer.

My shoulders and knees hurt.

This bedroom needs a dresser and a mirror.

Escaleras must be in the plural to agree with *las*. *Soñar, caminar,* and *andar* are all regular verbs and need to be used in their present tense. *Hombros* and *rodillas* must be in their plural forms.

CHAPTER 22

Glossary

acera—sidewalk
adiós—good-bye
afeitar(se)—to shave
aguardar—to wait
alegría—joy
amor—love
andar—to walk
anillo—ring
anteojos—eyeglasses
antiguo—old
arena—sand
auto—car
automóvil—car
avión—airplane
azul—blue

bajo—short
barca, barco—boat
barba—beard
bien—well
blanco—white
boda—wedding
bote—boat
bueno—good

cabello—hair
caer(se)—to fall

caja—box
calcetines—socks
callado—quiet
calle—street
cambiar—to change
caminar—to walk
camisa—shirt
carro—car
carta—letter (written message)
cartero—mailman
casamiento—wedding
cerca—near
chaqueta—coat
chico—small
ciego—blind
clavo—nail
coche—car
colegio—school
colorado—red
comprar—to buy
conocer—to know
contento—happy
correr—to run
corto—short
crecer—to grow
creer—to believe
cuadro—painting
cultivar—to grow
cumpleaños—birthday

débil—weak
descansar—to rest
día—day
Día de Acción de Gracias—Thanksgiving
diario—newspaper
dibujo—drawing
difícil—hard

Dios—God
doctor—physician
duro—hard

edificio—building
enviar—to send
escalera—stair
escritorio—desk
escuchar—to hear, listen
escuela—school
espejuelos—eyeglasses
esperanza—hope
esperar—to wait
esposa—wife
esposo—husband
estacionar(se)—to park
estrella—star

familia—family
feliz—happy
florero—vase
fuego—fire
fuerte—strong

gafas—eyeglasses
ganar—to win
grande—big, large
granja—farm

hasta luego—good-bye, see you later
hierro—iron
humo—smoke

irse—to leave

jarrón—vase
jugar—to play

lápiz—pencil
largo—long
leer—to read
lejos—far
letra—letter (of alphabet)
levantarse—to get up, stand
libro—book
limpio—clean
llegar—to arrive
luna—moon

madera—wood
malo, mal—bad
mandar—to send
mañana—morning
máquina—machine
mar—sea
marido—husband
medias—socks, stockings
médico—physician
mercado—market
mesa—table
miedo—fear
mirar—to look
montaña—mountain
morir—to die
mover(se)—to move
mudarse—to move
muerte—death

nacer—to be born
nacimiento—birth
nadar—to swim
Navidad(es)—Christmas
negocio—business
negro—black
noche—night

observar—to watch
odiar—to hate
oír—to hear
olvidar—to forget
oro—gold

pantalones—pants
papel—paper
pararse—to stand
partir—to leave
peinarse—to comb (one's hair)
pelo—hair
pensar—to think
pequeño—small
perder—to lose
periódico—newspaper
pesadilla—nightmare
plata—silver
playa—beach
policía—policeman
ponerse de pie—to stand

recordar—to remember
reloj—watch
río—river
rojo—red
ruido—noise

sábanas—sheets
saber—to know
saco—coat
salud—health
saludar—to greet
sentarse—to sit
silla—chair
sobre—envelope

sol—sun
soldado—soldier
sonrisa—smile
sucio—dirty
sueño—dream

trabajar—to work
tren—train
triste—sad

vacaciones—vacation
vecindario—neighborhood
vecino—neighbor
vender—to sell
ver—to see
vereda—sidewalk
vestirse—to dress (oneself)
viajar—to travel
viejo—old
viento—wind
vigilar—to watch

zapatos—shoes

NOTES

NOTES

NOTES

REA's Study Guides

Review Books, Refreshers, and Comprehensive References

Problem Solvers®

Presenting an answer to the pressing need for easy-to-understand and up-to-date study guides detailing the wide world of mathematics and science.

High School Tutors®

In-depth guides that cover the length and breadth of the science and math subjects taught in high schools nationwide.

Essentials®

An insightful series of more useful, more practical, and more informative references comprehensively covering more than 150 subjects.

Super Reviews®

Don't miss a thing! Review it all thoroughly with this series of complete subject references at an affordable price.

Interactive Flashcard Books®

Flip through these essential, interactive study aids that go far beyond ordinary flashcards.

Reference

Explore dozens of clearly written, practical guides covering a wide scope of subjects from business to engineering to languages and many more.

For our complete title list,
visit www.rea.com

Research & Education Association

REA's Test Preps
The Best in Test Preparation

- *REA "Test Preps" are **far more** comprehensive than any other test preparation series*
- *Each book contains full-length practice tests based on the most recent exams*
- ***Every** type of question likely to be given on the exams is included*
- *Answers are accompanied by **full** and **detailed** explanations*

REA publishes hundreds of test prep books. Some of our titles include:

Advanced Placement Exams (APs)
Art History
Biology
Calculus AB & BC
Chemistry
Economics
English Language &
    Composition
English Literature &
    Composition
European History
French Language
Government & Politics
Latin Vergil
Physics B & C
Psychology
Spanish Language
Statistics
United States History
World History

**College-Level Examination
    Program (CLEP)**
American Government
College Algebra
General Examinations
History of the United States I
History of the United States II
Introduction to Educational
    Psychology
Human Growth and Development
Introductory Psychology
Introductory Sociology
Principles of Management
Principles of Marketing
Spanish
Western Civilization I
Western Civilization II

SAT Subject Tests
Biology E/M
Chemistry
French
German
Literature
Mathematics Level 1, 2
Physics
Spanish
United States History

Graduate Record Exams (GREs)
Biology
Chemistry
General
Literature in English
Mathematics
Physics
Psychology

ACT - ACT Assessment

ASVAB - Armed Services
    Vocational Aptitude Battery

CBEST - California Basic Educa-
    tional Skills Test

CDL - Commercial Driver License
    Exam

COOP, HSPT & TACHS - Catholic High
    School Admission Tests

FE (EIT) - AM Exam

FTCE - Florida Teacher Certification
    Examinations

GED

GMAT - Graduate Management
    Admission Test

LSAT - Law School Admission Test

MAT - Miller Analogies Test

MCAT - Medical College Admission
    Test

MTEL - Massachusetts Tests for
    Educator Licensure

NJ HSPA - New Jersey High School
    Proficiency Assessment

NYSTCE - New York State Teacher
    Certification Examinations

PRAXIS PLT - Principles of
    Learning & Teaching Tests

PRAXIS PPST - Pre-Professional
    Skills Tests

PSAT/NMSQT

SAT

TExES - Texas Examinations of
    Educator Standards

THEA - Texas Higher Education
    Assessment

TOEFL - Test of English as a
    Foreign Language

USMLE Steps 1, 2 - U.S. Medical
    Licensing Exams

*For our complete title list,
visit www.rea.com*

Research & Education Association